D1122983

Atlas of European Values

TILBURG · UNIVERSITY

CENTRE FOR SCIENCE AND VALUES

European *Values* Study

Atlas of European Values

**Loek Halman, Ruud Luijkx
and Marga van Zundert**

Colophon

Authors	Loek Halman, Ruud Luijkx and Marga van Zundert
Editorial advice	Wil Arts
Texts	Marga van Zundert
	Text chapters on politics and religion: Ralf Bodelier
Layout and graphic design	Beelenkamp Ontwerpers, Tilburg
	Carla van den Ouweland
	Project management: Joost Beelenkamp
Maps and graphics	Coen Tuerlings, Tilburg
Photography	Joyce van Belkom, Breda
	Photo Dr. J.P. Balkenende: copyright RVD/foto Dijkstra
	Photo flags: European Commission, Audiovisual services
	Photo Satelite page 131: www.metoffice.com/satpics/latest_vis.html
Project management	Pieter Siebers, Office of Public and External Affairs, Tilburg University
Series editors	Wil Arts and Loek Halman
Printing	Drukkerij Wilco, Amersfoort
ISSN	1568-5926
ISBN	90 04 14460 9

Library of Congress Cataloging-in-Publication Data
The Atlas of European Values / Loek Halman, Ruud Luijkx and
Marga van Zundert.
p. cm. -- (European values studies, ISSN 1568-5926 ; v. 8)
Data based on surveys carried out in 1990-1991 by the European
Values Study (www.europeanvalues.nl), in 1995-1996 by the World
Values Survey (www.worldvaluessurvey.org), and in 1999-2000
Tilburg University in collaboration with Zentralarchiv für Empirische
Sozialforschung (ZA) in Cologne and the Netherlands Institute for
Scientific Information Services in Amsterdam (NIWI)
Includes bibliographical references.
ISBN 90-04-14460-9 (alk. paper)
1. Social values--Europe--Public opinion--Atlases. 2. Values--Europe-
Public opinion--Atlases. 3. Europeans--Attitudes--Atlases. 4. Public
opinion--Europe--Atlases. 5. Group identity--Europe--Atlases.
I. Halman, Loek. II. Luijkx, Ruud. III. Zundert, Marga van. IV.
European values studies (Leiden, Netherlands) ; v. 8.

HM681.A85 2005
303.3'72'09406049--dc22   20005047007

Copyright 2005 by Koninklijke Brill NV Leiden and Tilburg University,
the Netherlands

All rights reserved. No part of this publication may be reproduced,
translated, stored in a retrieval system, or transmitted in any form
or by any means, electronic, mechanical, photocopying, recording or
otherwise, without prior written permission from the publisher.

Authorization to photocopy items for internal or personal use is
granted by Brill provided that the appropiate fees are paid directly
to The Copyright Clearance Center, 222 Rosewood Drive, Suite 910
Danvers MA 0923, U.S.A. Fees are subject to change.
Printed in the Netherlands

Contents

Foreword

Values to build on

"There is nothing more essential than what we carry in our minds." These are the words of the Roman architect Marcus Vitruvius, best known as the author of De Architectura. One of the greatest principles he left us is that a construction - any construction - must reflect the measure of man.

For all those who work on the great European edifice, that principle should never be forgotten. After the Second World War, the European Union succeeded brilliantly at generating stability and prosperity. But that was not enough for people to identify closely with the European project. My generation grew up thinking of the European Communities as vehicles for economic cooperation. The other side of European integration, the community of individuals and values, was long neglected. Markets and money took precedence over man and morals. European integration was taking place behind the backs of the Europeans, so to speak.

But people are not just consumers and producers. Whoever takes the European Union seriously as a political project must consider "what we carry in our minds" - our values, ideas, dreams and convictions. Everything that binds us, despite all our differences. As immigration, cultural blending and enlargement give rise to new uncertainties, those binding forces are becoming even more important.

Since the early 1980s, this line of thought has informed the European Values Studies on which this Atlas of European Values is based. The initiators of this project were clearly ahead of their time.

In the last six months of 2004, the Dutch presidency of the European Union made European values a political priority for the first time. Prominent figures in the arts and sciences, politics, education and civil society met in a series of five international conferences to identify the meaning of common values for us Europeans.

The conclusions largely corresponded to the lessons from the European Values Studies. An astounding variety of people call Europe home and unite our continent in diversity. Their common ground is defined by the values of freedom, solidarity, equality, and respect for human rights and the rule of law. Freedom and democracy in Europe would be impossible without active civil society and public authorities that champion those values. Europe needs engaged citizens who claim a measure of responsibility for their society and take pride in its values and rich cultural heritage. Openness is a hallmark of European civilisation. New ideas have always been welcome here and that has always been Europe's strength. This is why we must not put up fences around our European identity.

Making European values visible is crucial for the vitality and success of the European project. Ultimately, that implies building bridges between our values and our policies.

This atlas is a treasure-trove of information on the wealth of opinions about Europe and the forces that bind us in spite of our differences. It advances the dialogue about what Europe stands for, a dialogue which is fundamental to European culture. For as Vitruvius said, "there is nothing more essential than what we carry in our minds."

Dr. Jan Peter Balkenende
Prime Minister of the Kingdom of the Netherlands

Prologue

Conscious of its spiritual and moral heritage, the European Union is founded on the indivisible, universal values of human dignity, freedom, equality and solidarity..."

Preamble, Charter Fundamental Rights of the Union,
Constitution of the European Union, 29 October 2004

Europe, the old world

The history of Europe starts with an ancient Greek myth. Young and beautiful Europa, the daughter of Agenor, once King of the city of Tyre (now in Lebanon), is abducted by the Greek supreme god Zeus. He transforms himself into a white bull and tempts her to jump on his back. He brings her to Crete, where he ravishes her on the shore of the continent that would bear their offspring and her name. However, when Europe was first mentioned by the Greeks, they did not mean Europe as we know it today. They merely referred to Hellas, the lands around the Aegean seas, the part of the Mediterranean that today lies between Greece and Turkey. The Greeks thought of Europe as a strong civilization concentrated in free, independent, and democratic city-states. The northern and western parts of Europe were not included and considered 'uncivilized'. The inhospitable climate made the inhabitants brave and warlike, but also uncouth and unthinking.
'Europe' was also a concept used in the Roman empire, but it was not used self-descriptively; Rome might have been in Europe, but it didn't consider itself to be European. The Roman Empire regarded itself as Mediterranean, not continental. From the start it included parts of Africa and Asia, only in later years it expanded over the Alps, first to the Iberian Peninsula, then into Gaul, Britain and the Rhine delta. The Roman Empire unified for the first time the larger part of the continent and left its traces predominantly in legislation. With the end of the Roman Empire the concept of Europe moved West. Western Europe had been a peripheral region of the Mediterranean civilization, but became the middle point of the new Europe, now united by Christendom. From Rome, to London, to Berlin, Christian-Judaic values were underlined and for the first time people of all nations could understand each other through churches' Latin. By 1300 Europe existed for the first time in history as an identifiable cultural entity and covers more or less the Europe as we know it today. But also today, Europe is not a well-defined geographical region. Some will intuitively include Turkey and Russia, others will draw the eastern borders before the Ural. Depending on the 'eye of the beholder' the continent counts between 450 and 800 million citizens, and between 25 and 40 nations of which five rank in the top ten of world's largest economies: Germany, UK, France, Italy and Spain. In total, Europe's economy ranks second or third in the world, after North America and before or after Asia, depending on the definitions taken.

Moulded

Europe is the proud father of some of the greatest assets of human heritage: liberty, democracy and humanism. And it is the birthplace of so many great statesmen, poets, artists, composers, scientists and philosophers. Aristotle, Mozart, Bach, Descartes, Erasmus, Molière, Shakespeare, Nietzsche, Van Gogh, Freud, Kant and Einstein, to name just a few. Nobody can deny Europe's tremendously culturally rich history, its famous architecture, music or poetry. Or as the contemporary philosopher George Steiner put it so elegantly "a landscape has been moulded, humanized by feet and hands. As in no other part of the globe the shores, fields, forests, hills of Europe, from La Coruña to Saint Petersburg, from Stockholm to Messina, have been shaped not so much by geological as by human-historical time...."
But despite all its glory, its great names and successes, Europe has also many dark periods to answer for: the crusades, colonialism and most recently the horrifying holocaust. Only sixty years ago, after the Second World War, Europe once again lay in ruins. Statesmen came together in an ultimate attempt to initiate lasting peace, and to end the terrible loss of lives. Robert Schuman, the foreign minister of France proposed tying up the steel and coal industry ensuring strong mutual interests between nations, a solid economic link that would make war and conflicts highly contra productive. The result was the European Coal and Steel Community, the forerunner to the European Union. The unification along economic lines was successful; it has brought peace and economic prosperity to its members over the past sixty years. However, not all of Europe took part in this process. The eastern part of the continent chose, or rather was made to choose communism as their political ideology and became part of the Soviet empire. Others were excluded for political reasons or decided that they were better off 'alone'. After the fall of the iron curtain in 1989, many East-European countries applied for membership of the union and ten have joined in recently; and another three will join in

soon. Furthermore, Europe is also considering Turkish membership. However, also in recent history Europe has not been able to prevent bloodshed on its territories. The war in former Yugoslavia meant another dark chapter in European history. Who are these Europeans who provide such a mixed blessing to humanity? How do they think? What values do they treasure? What binds them and what divides them? If one thing is certain, it is that these questions are not easily answered. Europe is a construction, a set of stories, images, resonances, collective memories, invented and carefully nurtured traditions. As said before, Europe ended in the German forests at one time, in the Urals at another. Most Europeans share the experience of living under Roman law, Christianity and the secular culture developed in the Age of Enlightenment. However, Roman law, Christianity and the Enlightenment have not shaped the values of every nation and all citizens in the same way and with the same depth in the course of time.

European spirit

In 2002, Romano Prodi, the President of the European Commission, installed a Reflection Group on the Spiritual and Cultural Dimension of Europe, consisting of twelve renowned Europeans - historians, philosophers, politicians, economists, social scientists and a writer. These twelve had the task of reflecting on the role that the most deep-rooted values of our shared historical background could play as the binding agent of fellowship and solidarity. Prodi stated "As the shadow of the Second World War becomes more distant in Europe's collective memory, the EU needs more than economic integration to hold it together."

However, these twelve scholars could not provide a solid core of European identity. "Every attempt to codify European values is inevitably confronted by a variety of diverging national, regional, ethnic, sectarian, and social understandings", reports Krzysztof Michalski. "This diversity of interpretation cannot be eliminated by a constitutional treaty, even if backed up by legislation and judicial interpretation".

European Unification - key data

1951 Six nations (Belgium, France, Germany, Italy, Luxembourg and The Netherlands) sign the Treaty of Paris establishing European Coal and Steel Community (ECSC).

1953 The procedure regulation of the European Court of Justice is published in the Official Journal of the ECSC. As of today appeals foreseen by the Paris Treaty can be placed to the Court.

1957 The treaties establishing the European Economic Community (EEC) and the European Atomic Energy Community (Euratom) are signed in Rome.

1958 The session setting up the European Parliamentary Assembly is held in Strasbourg, France.

1967 The institutions of the three European communities (ECSC, EEC and Euratom) are merged. From this point on, there is a single Commission and a single Council of Ministers as well as the European Parliament.

1972 The currency 'snake' is set up: the margin of fluctuation between their currencies is limited to 2.25%.

1973 Denmark, Ireland and the United Kingdom join the European Communities.

1979 First direct elections for the European Parliament.

1981 Greece joins the European Community.

1985 Greenland, which became a member of the European Community as part of Denmark, withdraws from the community.

1985 Schengen treaty signed for the elimination of internal border controls and free movement of persons.

1986 Spain and Portugal join the EC.

1992 Treaty of Maastricht: introduction of the political unity, new forms of co-operation between the member state governments - for example on defence, and in the area of "justice and home affairs". The EC becomes the European Union (EU). And the EU decides to go for economic and monetary union (EMU), involving the introduction of a single European currency managed by a European Central Bank.

1995 Austria, Finland and Sweden join the EU.

2002 The single currency - the euro - is introduced in twelve of the fifteen member countries: Belgium, Germany, Greece, Spain, France, Ireland, Italy, Luxembourg, the Netherlands, Austria, Portugal and Finland.

2004 Ten nations join the EU: Cyprus, the Czech Republic, Estonia, Hungary, Latvia, Lithuania, Malta, Poland, Slovakia and Slovenia, setting the total members of the Union on 25, representing 450 million people.

Source: www.europa.eu.int/abc/history/

European history in a nut shell

1000   1100   1200   1300   1400

GREEK REASONING
Around 500 BC, Europe, is for the first time, regarded as being a cultural entity. The Greeks think of Europe as a strong civilization concentrated in free, independent, and democratic city-states. However, their Europe is concentrated at the Mediterranean.

ROMAN LAW
In classical Rome, Europe was seen as a continent with an own identity. But the Romans didn't necessarily consider themselves to be European. The core of the Roman Empire was still the Mediterranean, although at its high point (around the year 100 AD) the empire included the Iberian peninsula and the larger parts of western Europe. The Roman Empire was an intensely legal society and in the course of several centuries, Roman jurists worked out a system of legal principles devised to protect both life and property. This law cherished citizenship and individual rights, equity and the common good.

CHRISTIANITY
In the Middle Ages, Christendom expanded gradually, however, the legacy of Greek and Roman Antiquity was preserved. Christendom not only brought a cultural shift but also a geographical. Western Europe that had been a peripheral region of the Mediterranean-based culture of classical Europe became integrated. Around 1300, Europe existed for the first time in history as an identifiable cultural entity. The church played a key role in establishing this homogeneity, Christendom expanded from Iceland and Spain to Hungary and Poland. Religion provided a common language, Latin, and a common source of values: the Bible. And the high Middle ages also brought a European intellectual elite. Italian scientists studied in Germany and Paris. Administrators went to the Netherlands and England. The most influential Christian idea in the history of Europe has probably been that of the equality of every person before God in heaven.

Still, despite such difficulties of definition, there can be no doubt that there exists a common European cultural space: a variety of traditions, ideals and aspirations, often intertwined and at the same time in tension with one another. These traditions, ideals and aspirations bring us together in a shared context and make us 'Europeans'. In 2004, another quest to find the European spirit was made by the Nexus Instituut affiliated with Tilburg University. The Institute launched a series of conferences entitled: Europe, a beautiful idea? as part of the Dutch presidency of the European Union. The opening lecture was made by George Steiner with an essay entitled "The idea of Europe". He wrote "Even a child in Europe bends under the weight of the past. What can anyone of us add to the immensities of the European past? [...] To be a European is to attempt to negotiate, morally, intellectually and existentially the rival ideals, claims, praxis of the city of Socrates and that of Isaiah". With these definitions of the European spirit we have not come much further than what the French poet and essayist Paul Valéry wrote in 1919 in La crise de l'Esprit: "A European is anyone who is influenced by three cultural patterns: the universal legal order of Rome, Christianity and Greek reason". Yet, despite a perhaps rather indistinctive European culture and identity, the European Union has grown to 25 member states and 450 million citizens in 2004, who live in a rather stable, peaceful, free and relatively wealthy society where large majorities believe that unification is a good thing (europa.eu.int/comm/public_opinion/). From that perspective, Europe still consistently follows the trajectory of its founding father Robert Schuman who in 1950 argued at the cradle of the union: "Europe will not be made all at once, or according to a single plan. It will be built through concrete achievements which first create a de facto solidarity".

Furthermore, seen from within Europe, the differences that separate German from Italian culture are easy enough to perceive. Viewed, however, from Japan, those differences will seem less obvious than the similarities. Anyone who walks through Rome, London or Prague will recognize Europe in the architecture and in the people. Europeans do have the habit of stressing their cultural differences, instead of their similarities.

ABSOLUTISM

The age of absolutism started in about 1650. Europe saw the gradual erosion of local power and autonomy and the rise of national legislation and civil bureaucracies resulting in absolute and centralized power of the national government and the monarchy.

MODERNITY

After the French and industrial revolution modernity brings the rise of industrial capitalism and parliamentary democracy in Europe, and the transformation of religious beliefs into economic and political ethics: liberalism, socialism and nationalism. The most important of these ideologies was democracy. Resulting in the 1789 Déclaration des droits de l'homme.

UNIFICATION

After the horrors of World Wars I and II, the need for peace urged European nations towards unification. In 1951, the European Union is established by six European countries (Belgium, France, Germany, Italy, Luxembourg and The Netherlands). The union grows to 25 members and 450 million citizens in the year 2004 (see also EU key data on page 9).

| 500 | 1600 | 1700 | 1800 | 1900 | 2000 |

RENAISSANCE, REFORMATION AND HUMANISM

At the end of the Middle ages, around 1500, the Renaissance, reformation and humanism created a new vision of man in Europe. The new European is sovereign in the world and, with his reason and creative powers, also able to penetrate any secret, and make anything he invented. Without losing their beliefs in the basic tenets of Christianity the humanist thinkers emphasized more individualistic and more secular values.

ENLIGHTENMENT

The treaty of Utrecht in 1713 provided the last major occasion on which public reference was made to the Christian commonwealth. After that, the awareness of a European opposed to a Christian community gained the upper hand. The scientific revolutions of the seventeenth and the Enlightenment of the eighteenth centuries brought about changes in the structure of European thought itself: systematic doubt, empirical and sensory verification, the abstraction of human knowledge into separate sciences, and the view that the world functions like a machine. Subsequently, the industrial revolution irrevocably changed human labour, consumption, family structure, social structure, and even the very soul and thoughts of the individual. During the Enlightenment the term Europe became more than a geographical concept. Europe was associated with civilization. Voltaire described Europe as a kind of great republic divided into several states all based on the same religious foundation and the same principle of public law and politics.

NATIONALISM

In the nineteenth century a specifically national sense of citizenship emerged. This resulted in the idea of the welfare state but also lead to nationalism that proved to be very destructive. Europe tore itself in pieces in two world wars (1914-1918 and 1939-1945), that made sixty to eighty million victims and simply eradicated the equation of Europe with civilization.

The atlas

At the end of the 1970s a small group of social researchers headed by Ruud de Moor from Tilburg University and Jan Kerkhofs from Catholic University of Leuven initiated a research project to measure European values. Initially, they were mostly interested in finding out if Europe was still culturally unified as it had once been under the influence of Christianity. The central research question was: Have traditional norms and values been shaken fundamentally in modern times? To study values they organized a major cross-national survey in 1981 in the fifteen European Union member states.

The survey covered the main life domains. Questions included were: How important is family in your life? How important is God, work, or politics? But the survey also tapped people's level of tolerance, their solidarity, sexual attitudes, civic engagement, faith and ethics. The research project was called the European Values Study and in order to track changes in values repeat surveys were organised in 1990 and 1999/2000. The initiative was followed by non-European scientists and the project expanded into the World Values Survey.

Today, the data of the European Values Study and the World Values Survey have proved to be a gold mine for social researchers. Because of the wide range of issues addressed in the questionnaire, researchers from various backgrounds and different scientific disciplines can use and analyze the data which is freely accessible on the internet (www.europeanvalues.nl and www.worldvaluessurvey.org). This atlas summarizes the results of the European Values Study in 2000. It presents the ideas and believes of European people in graphs, charts and maps in such a way that they are also accessible for the non-specialist. What does the atlas tell us about Europeans? First of all, the charts and maps underline the earlier observations and conclusions that there is no such thing as a clear set of European values. Democracy, freedom, equality, human dignity and solidarity are underlined by almost all Europeans. But, although some may have been first formulated by Europeans, to call such values universal or perhaps western 'European' would be self-centred, arrogant, or at least pretentious. We recommend this atlas as an accessible presentation of European values, a book to browse to discover Europe's unique diversity; and to remind that 'God lies in the detail'.

Europe

A substantial majority of Europeans applaud Europe's unification. However, very few experience truly warm feelings when seeing its blue flag fluttering or hearing its (unofficial) hymn Beethoven's 'Ode to joy' play. The citizens of Europe have a rational-based attitude towards the Union. They seem to enthusiastically embrace the economic benefits, but unification doesn't result in a feeling of being European, let alone a feeling of European pride.

In fact over 800 million people could call themselves European. The eastern borders of the continent are rather diffuse. Russia, Belarus and Ukraine are often regarded as part of Europe, but from a geographical point of view Turkey, Armenia, Georgia, Azerbaijan and perhaps also Greenland have as much right to this qualification. Greenland in fact once was a member of the European Community (1973-1985), but decided to withdraw after becoming independent from Denmark. The Islanders choose to look for closer contact with their North-American neighbours. Turkey and Azerbaijan don't share the Christian roots like the rest of the continent does, and are therefore often considered 'too eastern' to belong to Europe. However, the people of Albania and Bosnia are also predominantly Muslim. Perhaps European citizenship is only indisputable for the 435 million people living in one of the 25 EU-member countries.

Shared roots

But how many people actually feel European? According to the European Values Studies (see page 17) very few, even in the EU-member countries.
On average less than 5% of these citizens consider themselves to be foremost European; a figure that cannot even match the percentage that primarily think of themselves as a 'world citizen'. Thus, although there appears to be a European identity as is proven by the 'exclusion' of certain countries not many treasure it.
But why is this? According to

sociologists identification is primarily a feeling of belonging and self-consciousness. Members of even the smallest nation will never know most of their fellow-countrymen or meet them, yet they feel connected and show a high level of solidarity. This is thought to be the result of shared roots: shared memories and experiences, a common language, culture and feeling of destiny. First of all the shared roots lead to national pride. Although not all countries in Europe are nation-states, people almost unanimously say they are (very) proud of their country (see page 21).
Europeans do share a lot of common history: the decline and fall of the Roman Empire, the rise of Christianity, the Enlightenment, Humanism, industrialisation etc. Yet, Europe's rich civilization

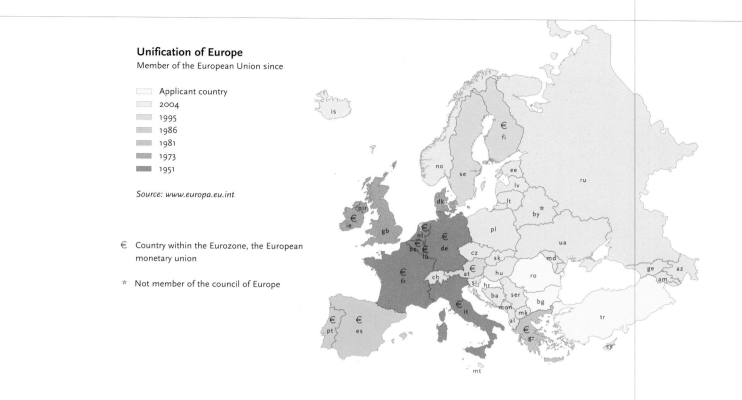

Unification of Europe

Member of the European Union since

Applicant country
2004
1995
1986
1981
1973
1951

Source: www.europa.eu.int

€   Country within the Eurozone, the European
     monetary union

*   Not member of the council of Europe

process has not shaped the values of every inhabitant in the same way and the same depth. Europe is a complicated mosaic of old and new natural, political, linguistic and religious dividing lines that separate people. Remember that in the Middle Ages, Europe's 80 million people lived in 200 states, would-be states, fiefdoms and state-like organizations. Modern European countries are in many instances combinations of these rudimentary states, where little cultural cohesion occurs. The recent civil wars in Bosnia, Croatia and Serbia are sad illustrations of this fact.

National pride

Considering Europe's cultural diversity, the European Union may be called a surprising success. Today the Union counts 25 member states and unifies a majority of all European citizens. The unification started shortly after the Second World War, which left the continent ruined and divided, but with a strong consciousness of 'never again'. Despite this large moral foundation, unification was instead sought via economic and political lines.

The Union started out as the European Coal and Steel Community joining seven highly industrialized countries by mutual financial and economic interests. This strategy succeeded in preventing conflicts in its member states and realizing considerable welfare.

But for Europeans, nation comes first, then Europe. Europe has only been accepted in an instrumental and utilitarian way; no emotional or affective attachment exists towards the Union. Europeans perceive themselves foremost as French, Italian or Polish. They cherish their language, their habits and national culture. In many ways they see the Union even as a threat. Often legislation conflicts revolve around cultural habits: the bullfights in Spain, soft-drugs policy in the Netherlands, bank secrecy in Luxembourg etc. This rational-based European citizenship leads also to strange apparent contradictions, for example 71% of the Greeks find EU-membership a good thing, but the same percentage have no confidence in the Union.

And whereas only 7% of Russians feel European, two-third of the population wants to join the Union.

Feeling European

Globalization by age

The percentage of Europeans who feel most connected with their town, region or country versus the percentage who feel they first belong to Europe or the world according to age

local
global

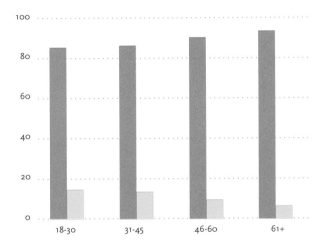

Globalization by education

The percentage of Europeans who feel most connected with their town, region or country versus the percentage who feel they first belong to Europe or the world according to level of education.

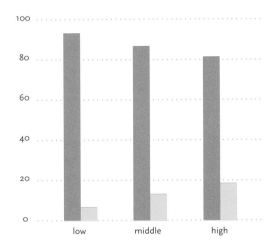

Eurosceptism

Percentage of people who indicate Europe as the geographical group they belong to the least

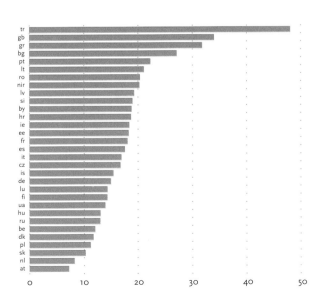

European solidarity

Percentage of people who feel concerned with the living conditions of their fellow Europeans

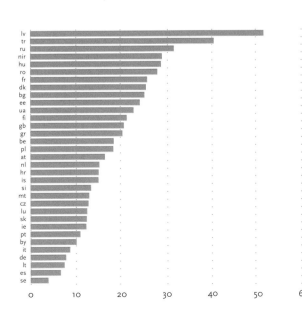

Nearly half of the Turks and a third of the British answer that they belong
the least to Europe when they are asked to choose between town,
region, country, Europe or the world

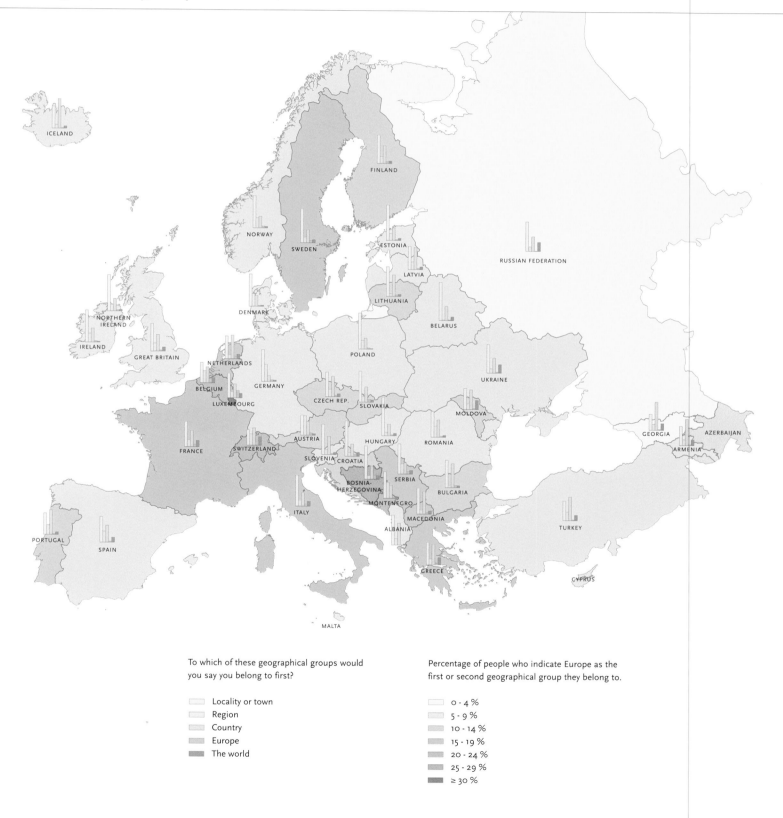

To which of these geographical groups would
you say you belong to first?

- Locality or town
- Region
- Country
- Europe
- The world

Percentage of people who indicate Europe as the
first or second geographical group they belong to.

- 0 - 4 %
- 5 - 9 %
- 10 - 14 %
- 15 - 19 %
- 20 - 24 %
- 25 - 29 %
- ≥ 30 %

Confidence in the European Union

Taking Europe's temperature

As of 1973, the European Union examines the support for the union among its citizens twice a year. The data of these Eurobarometers, are freely available and are one of the most comprehensive statistical sources on confidence in European institutions within the Union. One downside of the Eurobarometer however, is that it only includes member and applicant countries. The Eurobarometer of 1973 thus covered the 15 'oldest' members from Western, Northern and Southern Europe. Today, the barometer also includes the Eastern European countries that entered the EU in 2003 and the applicant countries, thus including almost 30 European nations. The Eurobarometer shows convincingly that over the last thirty years, a majority of the member state citizens agreed with the membership of the European Union. The statement that membership is a bad thing

is only endorsed by circa 15% of the EU-citizens. The people of the 15 'old' member countries regard freedom-of-movement and the Euro as the most positive aspects of the European Union. For the new member countries (Cyprus, the Czech Republic, Estonia, Hungary, Latvia, Lithuania, Malta, Poland, Slovakia and Slovenia) freedom-of-movement is by far the most positive aspect. The applicant countries add economic prosperity and social protection as important benefits of eventual membership of the Union. All-time high support for Union membership, 72%, was recorded in the spring of 1991. In the mid nineties, public support for the Union dropped sharply to reach an all-time low of 46% in the spring of 1997. The Gulf War, the economic crises, the debate on the Maastricht Treaty, the war in Yugoslavia and the inclusion of three relatively euro-skeptic countries (Sweden, Finland and Austria) are the most

probable reasons. In autumn 2004 the Union support rose to 56%. In most of the 15 'old' member countries the support for the Union has not changed dramatically since they joined the EU. Greece, Portugal and Ireland are the exceptions, here support has risen substantially; only in Great Britain has support dropped significantly. The support for membership in the applicant countries is high. 71% of Turkish citizens believe that EU-membership is a good thing, so do 70% of Romanians and 65% of Bulgarians. For Croatia, the fourth applicant country, no data is available. At the moment, the citizens of Luxembourg are the largest supporters of the Union (85% believes membership is a good thing), followed by the Irish (77%) and the Dutch (75%). The United Kingdom has the most euro-sceptic citizens, yet the supporters (38%) still outnumber the opponents (22%). Other euro-

sceptic countries are Latvia (40% pro, 14% contra) and Malta (45% pro, 17% contra). A majority of the current 250 million European Union citizens feel that they benefit from their country being a member. However, intra-member differences are large: 87% of the Irish belief they benefit, against 36% of the Swedes. In Sweden, Great Britain, Cyprus and Austria the people who are of the opinion that they don't benefit from the membership outnumber those who do believe they profit. The European Parliament, Commission and Central Bank tend to be trusted by the member state citizens, as is the Court of Justice. The confidence in these institutions is the highest in the 15 'old' member countries; the new member states and especially the candidate countries have less faith in the European Unions' institutions and bodies.
Source: europa.eu.int/comm/public_opinion/index_en.htm.

Confidence of EU-member states

Trust in the European Union for member and applicant states ordered according to length of membership.
Scale 1 (No confidence at all) - 4 (A great deal of confidence)

- 1951
- 1973
- 1981
- 1986
- 1995
- 2004
- Applicant

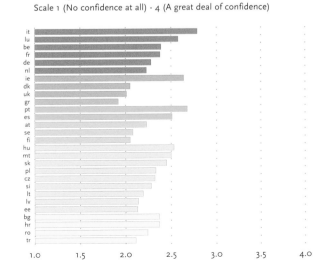

The Albanians have the highest confidence in the European Union:
41% have a great deal of confidence and another 42% have quite a lot of confidence
Of the member states the Italians show the most confidence, the Greek the least

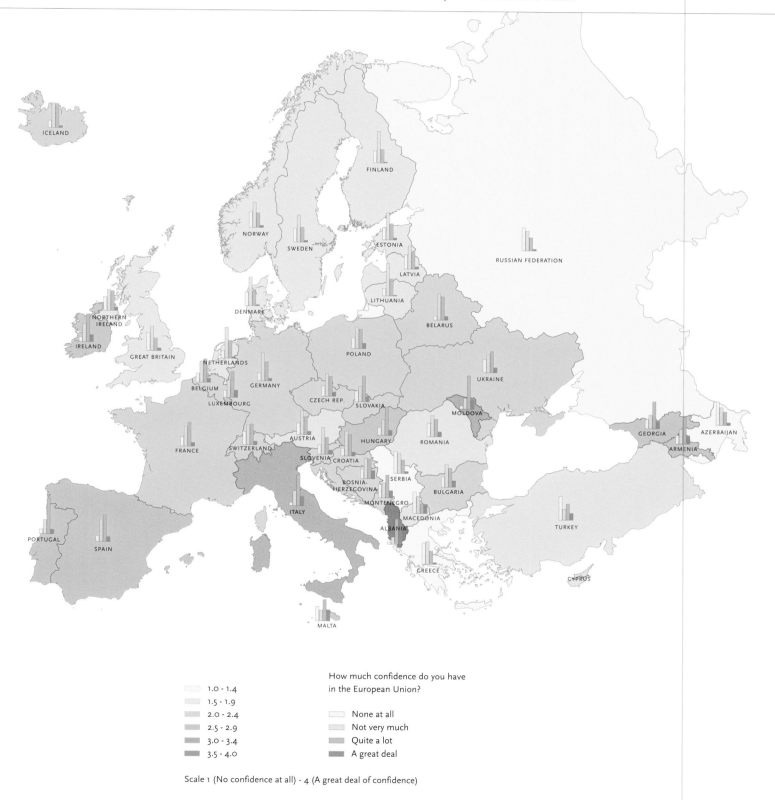

1.0 - 1.4	
1.5 - 1.9	
2.0 - 2.4	
2.5 - 2.9	
3.0 - 3.4	
3.5 - 4.0	

How much confidence do you have
in the European Union?

None at all
Not very much
Quite a lot
A great deal

Scale 1 (No confidence at all) - 4 (A great deal of confidence)

National pride

3.00 - 3.09
3.10 - 3.19
3.20 - 3.29
3.30 - 3.39
3.40 - 3.49
3.50 - 3.59
3.60 - 3.69
3.70 - 3.79

Scale 1 (Not at all proud) - 4 (Very proud)

National pride on the European isles

National pride is the positive affect that the inhabitants feel
towards their own country: They prefer their home country
above any other and they feel attached to it. However, there
seem to be as many ways to feel pride in a country as there
are individuals. Some people are proud of their country's
position in the world, others praise their country's social
security system, and yet others are proud when the national
football team performs well.

Research shows that the degree of national pride depends
to a certain extent on a nation's political history, a country's
economic and cultural achievements and its current position in
the world community. National pride appears to be greatest in
stable, established, well-developed democracies and
low in countries divided by ethnic conflict, and nations with
war guilt. But all these factors can only partly explain people's
national pride.

Within Europe, the citizens of island-states such as Iceland and
Malta are comparatively prouder of their country. Insularity has
been put forward as an explanation, as has scale. Both factors
enable citizens to know each other well, to value each others'
qualities and to build national unity.

National pride on the islands by age
Scale 1 (Not at all proud) - 4 (Very proud)

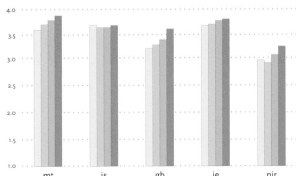

18 - 30
31 - 45
46 - 60
61+

Of the Lithuanians only 60% are proud of their country, the lowest score in Europe;
in 17 of the 43 countries more than half of the citizens say they are very proud of their country

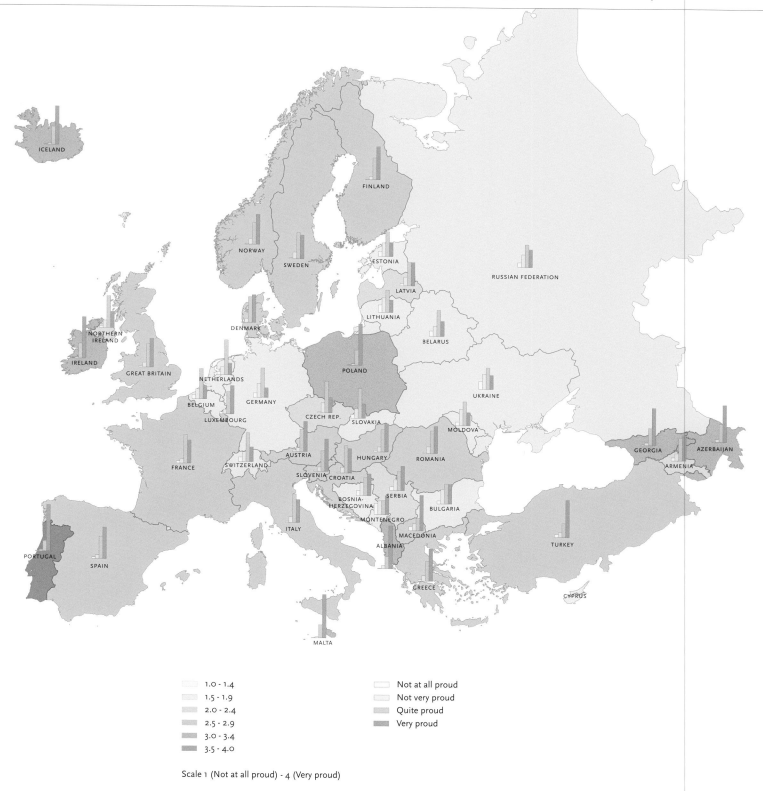

	1.0 - 1.4		Not at all proud
	1.5 - 1.9		Not very proud
	2.0 - 2.4		Quite proud
	2.5 - 2.9		Very proud
	3.0 - 3.4		
	3.5 - 4.0		

Scale 1 (Not at all proud) - 4 (Very proud)

EU and loss of culture

The European Union and unification can be viewed as a possible threat towards national identity and culture. In fact, the Eurobarometer shows that about 30% of the citizens fear cultural loss because of EU-membership. The European Values Studies put forward two opinions on the influence of the Union on national identity in six European countries (Austria, Italy, Lithuania, Czech Republic, Slovakia and Belarus). The statements were: A; If the European member states were truly to be united, this would mean the end of their national, historical and cultural identities. Their national economic interest would also be sacrificed, and B; Only a true united Europe can protect its states' national, historical and cultural identities and their national economic interests from the challenges of superpowers.

The support for statement B was higher than for A, in all six countries but Lithuania. In Italy, the support for statement B is most pronounced. However, statement B only just 'wins' in Austria, Czech Republic, Slovakia and Belarus, apparently the Europeans are not sure which way the scales will tip: will the EU turn out to be a keeper of the national cultural heritage and identity or will it squander away its treasures?

National pride in Europe by age
Scale 1 (Not at all proud) - 4 (Very proud)

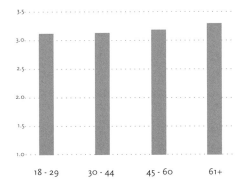

National pride in Europe by sex
Scale 1 (Not at all proud) - 4 (Very proud)

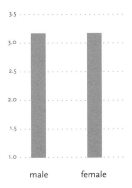

National pride in Germany by age
Scale 1 (Not at all proud) - 4 (Very proud)

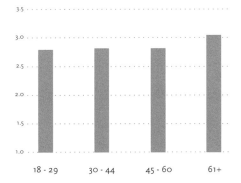

National pride in Europe by level of education
Scale 1 (Not at all proud) - 4 (Very proud)

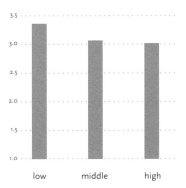

Despite their economic strength and leading position within the European community, Germany ranks very low on national pride. The reason is apparent, German citizens still feel guilty about their nation's attitude and actions during World War II. National guilt is noticeable even among the younger generation; the idea of 'national pride' has become an emotionally charged term.

*"There is a strong need for an European civil society.
Europe cannot be an ideal when its design is restricted
to a market and a state."*

Wim van de Donk
Professor of Public Administration

"Europe is a complex continent; dynamic and diverse, full of history and subtle nuances. Being a European is therefore never a simple, nor an obvious matter. Being a European will, for example, never be as straightforward as being a German or an American. Yet, travelling through Europe, I feel the continent everywhere. One can sense her spirit in Catalonia and recognize her values in the young Slovenians building up a new society on the Balkan ruins. Throughout Europe democracy, freedom and human rights are advocated. However, the most specific European values are, perhaps, rooted in Christianity and humanism: freedom, mutual respect and solidarity, these are the key values that have to be reconciled and balanced in the over-arching perspective of human dignity and brotherhood. Europe's unification started in the early fifties with the establishment of the European Coal and Steel Community. The community indeed tightly linked the economic interests of the coal and steel industry, but this was, of course, merely a pragmatic pretext. The true aim of the ECSC was to establish a far higher ideal: putting an end to the frequent and bloody wars that had divided the continent for so long.

However, as a result of the chosen strategy the further project 'Europe' had been defined dominantly along economic and political lines. We have formed a common European market, a common currency, and some kind of government and parliament. All very praiseworthy initiatives, but it will not be enough. While building 'political institutions' and a monetary union, we forgot that we need more to create a truly European society. There is no real European public space. There is no European newspaper or news channel. Europe misses out in the third sector while these are the organisations that make up a vivid society resulting in the creation of a sense of community and group identity. It is, to be honest, even worse. The two dominant parts of the European reality, the state and the market, tend to suffocate the civil societies that still exist at the national and regional levels, that magic domain where citizens reconcile their personal ambitions with the endeavours of their communities. Economy and administration have an inherent tendency to strive towards harmonization and equalization; people increasingly start to perceive Europe as a threat instead of the cradle of their traditions and culture. These are after all both rooted in civil society, A flourishing civil society can act as a natural buffer towards this 'threat'. Citizens can accept and tolerate differences and variety as they have an excellent perception of what is truly important in life, more so than voters or consumers who are often driven by fear and by short-term goals. Thus, civil society may provide the necessary resilience and flexibility in our European community. It is therefore high time that we look beyond the euro and revive the 'old' aspirations and ideals.

Trenches

How does one establish a blooming European civil society? This is certainly not an easy question, and we may need some miracles to get there. The European constitution is a good initiative as it reflects upon values and ideals, the true fundamentals for unification. It also establishes a moral basis for negotiations with possible new members of the Union. Negotiations about membership are and should be far more than a bargaining game about national budget deficits and agricultural subsidies. Of course these kinds of bargaining games are necessary, but they must not dominate the discourses. Again, this has become evident from the ongoing discussions about Turkey's entry into the EU. Another step in the right direction has been Europe's open coordination initiative which provides room for more variety and differences in political decision making processes, and that also recognizes that the European project is, essentially, not about standardization and homogenisation, but about variety and diversity. This method also provides more possibilities for an active participation of societal organizations in political and democratic decision making. Indeed, it transcends the ideal of democracy beyond the mere idea of a state. Furthermore, the European Union should become much more active in the cultural sector, for example, by enlarging the European film fund, by creating exchange of popular and regional culture or by stimulating a European news channel. There seems to be a kind of taboo about such initiatives, but creating a European public space is at least as important as creating a European Parliament. Finally, personal encounters with Europe's cultural diversity should be encouraged. Conventional wisdom is that as long as people talk to each other mutual problems will straighten themselves out; troubles really start when people stop looking into each other's eyes. A single visit to the Ieper trenches in Flanders will convince everyone that Europe is not an option, but a necessity. We need to create this European civil society; the alternative is cynicism and a victory of the calculating citizen. Europe will be disjointed, an incoherent soulless bureaucratic institution in which no one feels at home. Perhaps, this visit to the Ieper trenches should be made mandatory for all youngsters in Europe. They will immediately recognize the importance of hope and see that miracles do happen."

Prof. Dr. Wim van de Donk is a professor of Public Administration and Third Sector Organizations at The Tilburg School for Politics and Public Administration, Law Faculty, Tilburg University, the Netherlands, and Chairman of the Netherlands' Scientific Council for Government Policy in The Hague. Contact: donk@wrr.nl

Family

Today few households in Europe consist of the traditional male bread-winner, female housekeeper and several children. Yet as it comes to family values, Europeans come out surprisingly conservative. 'Married-with-children' is the preferred lifestyle for an overwhelming majority, despite the liberating sixties, emancipation and individualization.

Within Europe the traditional nuclear family type, considered as two adults with dependent children and a sole male bread-winner, has declined dramatically. Dual-income and one-parent families, predominantly female, are increasingly common. Evidence is found in demographic figures: the number of marriages has declined, the number of divorces is rising and the average household size is reduced to around 2.5.

Two explanations have been proposed for the 'fall' of the traditional family: women's participation in the workforce and individualization. In all contemporary European societies women have started in jobs outside the household. Although for many women this move will have been more or less an economical necessity, this work represents a means of independence and emancipation. And indeed, the growing number of women working outside their homes has changed not only the

outlook on women's roles in society, but on gender roles in general.

Individualization
The decline of the traditional family has also been interpreted as a result of ongoing individualization and modernization. In today's society, the individual has become free and independent from the traditional, social and religious institutions. People can choose their lifestyle and can make their decisions upon personal interests and values. A development that has resulted in a more individualistic patterning of family life. The classical family may be outdated, but the European Values Study clearly shows that family is considered the most important domain in life (page 127). Indeed, family is regarded as of far greater importance than work, friends, religion or free time. In this respect family remains the corner-stone of society. This is even true

in the Scandinavian countries where the demographic trends seem to indicate the disappearance of the traditional family. Family has become a wider concept than the traditional household or marriage. Today the term includes couples living together, single parents, gay couples with or without children and 'reconstituted' families - households including children of earlier relationships of one or more of the adult members. Today all alternatives to traditional marriages are associated with the term family.

Cuddling fathers
The participation of married women in the labour market has changed the husbands' traditional family role as the sole breadwinner. However, the redistribution of economic responsibility has not necessarily been accompanied by a redistribution of domestic and caring responsibilities.
Men have been hesitant to accept

childrearing and housekeeping tasks. The traditional view of child-rearing and housekeeping as a female responsibility is still strong in Europe. The wife's participation in the workforce seems accepted, but only as long as it does not interfere with her childcaring tasks. Women often work part-time or choose jobs that they can easily combine with childcaring tasks. As the fathers' breadwinner status is no longer either neces-sary or central to the family, their roles as fathers must be renego-tiated within a new gender order. An order which seems almost to exclude their significance and importance. Moreover, there are few or no role models for the new, involved father except for being 'a totally different father than my own'. Again differences around Europe are large. Women's parti-cipation in the work force varies and has caused the redistribution of household tasks which varies according to the amount of labour

Total fertility rate

The average number of children that would be born per woman if all women lived to the end of their child-bearing years and bore children (The total fertility rate is a more direct measure of the level of fertility than the crude birth rate, since that refers to births per woman).

1.00 - 1.19
1.20 - 1.39
1.40 - 1.59
1.60 - 1.79
1.80 - 1.99
2.00 - 2.19
2.20 - 2.40

Source: CIA World Factbook 2003

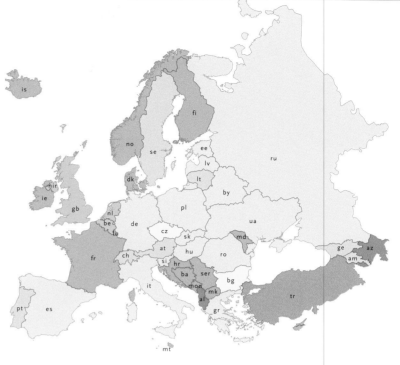

The importance of family

Percentage of Europeans who consider family .....

0
2
12
86

Not at all important
Not important
Quite important
Very important

Percentage of Europeans who consider more emphasis on family life .....

1
6
93

Good
Don´t mind
Bad

the wife partakes in outside the home. Scandinavian countries are often regarded as a foreland of the new father role, whereas the southern 'masculine' countries cling to the traditional father role.

Family growth

Thanks to economic welfare, contraceptives and individual freedom, having children is no longer a necessity, nor inevitable. Children have merely become an option, as is the choice of not having children. The acceptance of a childless life has increased, but this does not mean that childlessness is considered an ideal situation. On the contrary, the number of people who do not want children is negligible throughout Europe; at least one or possibly two children are considered ideal. Especially in Eastern Europe where a majority considers parenthood a necessity for a fulfilling life (page 29) and children are considered an important success factor in mar-

riage. However, the number of children within one household has significantly decreased since the 1960s. In 1960 the fertility rate in Europe was around 3, however it is well below 2 at the moment, with the highest rates in Albania, Turkey and Azerbaijan and the lowest in Bulgaria, Czech Republic and Latvia. Norway took active measures in response to the fall in fertility rate in the 1980s. The country extended the paid maternity leave from 18 weeks to one year, provided an adequate supply of kindergartens, arranged public care for children entering school and improved living standards for families with small children through public transfers. Since then the fertility rate has stabilized at 1.8. A relatively high level in Europe, but not enough to change the prospect of population decline.

Children

Economically useless, emotionally priceless

Today, children have become an option. They are no longer an inevitability, an economic necessity, a provision for old age or a duty to God. Having children and the actual number of children are a matter of personal and free choice. And during the last century, the 'ideal' number of children has dropped from about four or more to two.

Also the 'image' of children has shifted. Children have become 'little angels', requiring and deserving high investments and intense emotional involvement from their parents. Where the father used to be the centre of the family, home has slowly transformed into a child-centred haven. As a consequence, the distance between child and parent has reduced significantly. And childrearing has become more demanding. A child needs personal attention for its emotional and social development, not only disciplinary supervision.

The change of the father-centred family into a children-centred family is also evident from the European Values Studies. Europeans believe that parents should do their utmost best for their children, even at the cost of their own well-being. And the prevailing view is that both a father and a mother are necessary for a child in order to grow up happily. Here, individualism meets its limitations: as soon as children are involved, people appear reluctant to adhere to individualistic stances, instead they remain loyal to the traditional family patterns. It seems as if children and in particularly their well-being, are becoming an important, if not the most important, issue in the domain of family.

Both a father and a mother

Percentage of people with and without children who agree with the statement that a child needs a home with both a mother and a father to grow up happily.

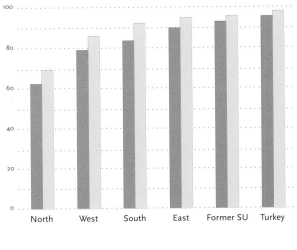

Without children
With children

A single mother

Percentage of men and women who approve of a mother who chooses to have a child on her own without having a stable relationship, according to age.

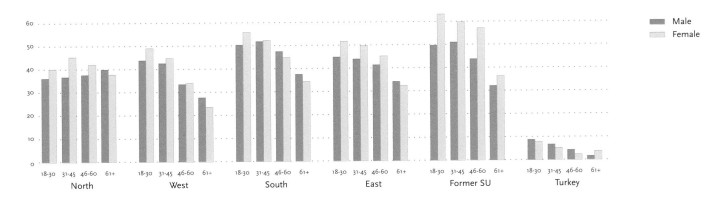

Male
Female

90% of the Latvian people find that men and women need children to fulfil their lives; less than 8% of the Dutch agree with them

Percentage of people who agree with the statement
"A woman needs children to fulfil her life"

Percentage of people who agree with the statement
"A man needs children to fulfil his life"

Percentage of people who agree with the statement
"A child needs a home with both a father and
a mother to grow up happily"

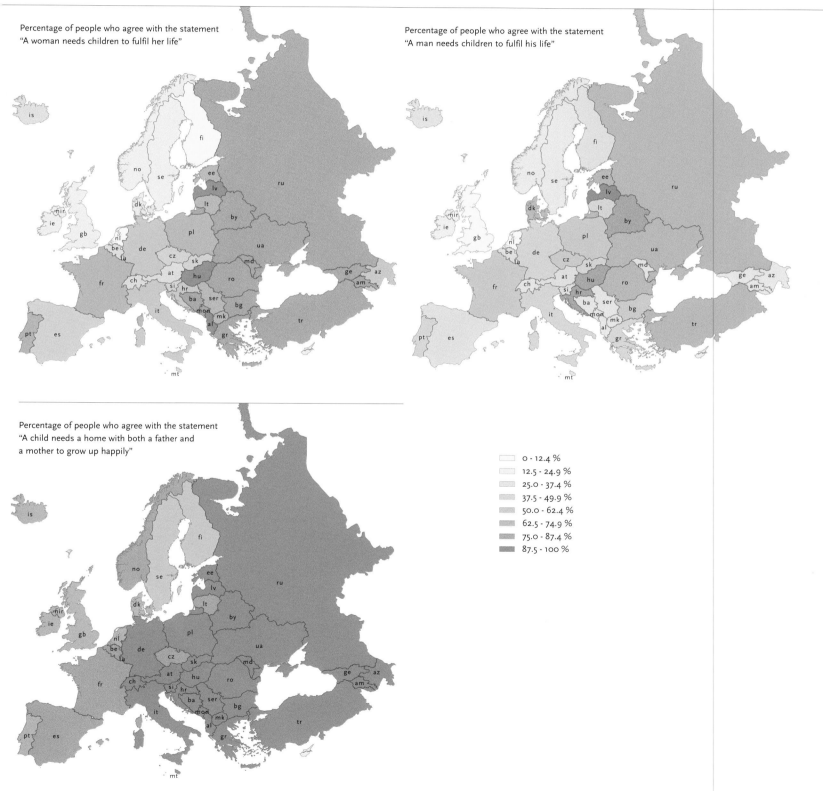

	0 - 12.4 %
	12.5 - 24.9 %
	25.0 - 37.4 %
	37.5 - 49.9 %
	50.0 - 62.4 %
	62.5 - 74.9 %
	75.0 - 87.4 %
	87.5 - 100 %

Marriage

Marriage is outdated
Percentage of people who *disagree* with the statement
"Marriage is outdated"

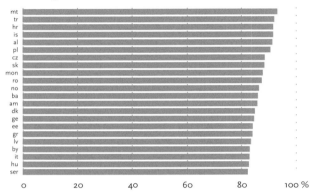

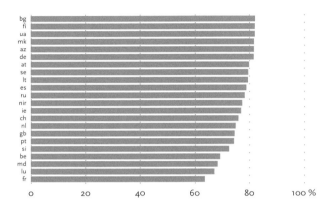

Divorce: incidence versus justifiability

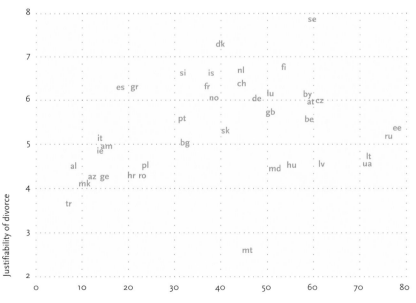

Divorce rate (as percentage of marriages in 2001)

Source: Statistical yearbook of the Economic Commission for Europe 2003

Analysis of the EVS-data revealed three characteristics that are significantly related to the public's approval of divorce on the state level: frequency of church attendance, type of welfare regime, and divorce rate - as is displayed here.

The higher the divorce rate in a society the more likely people are to tolerate it in their community. This finding confirms social structure theories which assume that similarities in attitudes within groups stem from common life experiences and situations that people encounter. However, the effect of a country's divorce rate disappears if one takes into account compositional differences between populations, that is to say when differences are levelled out by sex, age, level of education, and personal experience with divorce. Thus, a country's higher permissiveness of divorce is more the result of people's personal experiences with divorce than of the actual divorce rate in the country.

Europeans don't find marriage an outdated institution
Faithfulness is unanimously considered of utmost importance
for a successful marriage

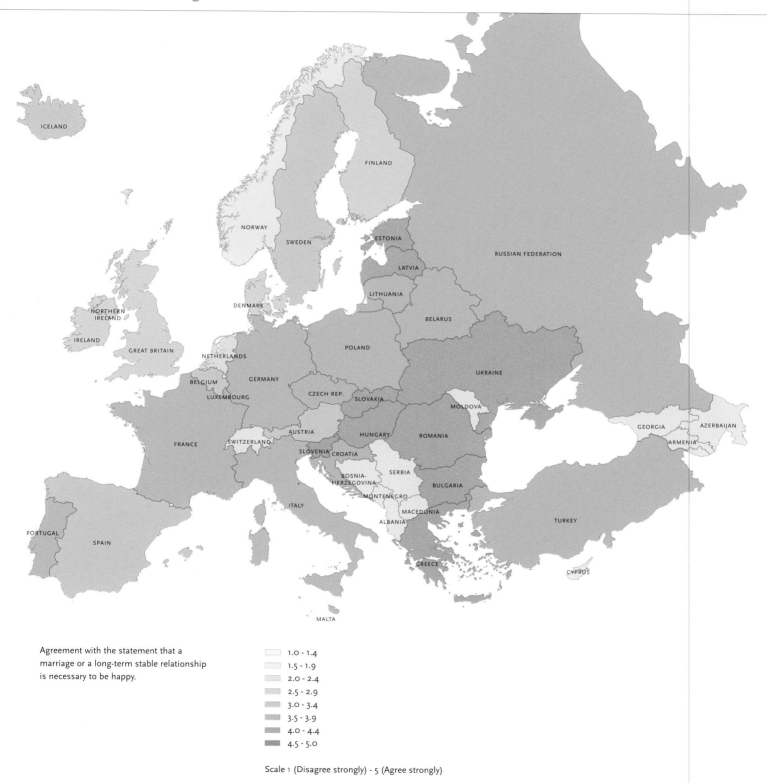

Agreement with the statement that a
marriage or a long-term stable relationship
is necessary to be happy.

	1.0 - 1.4
	1.5 - 1.9
	2.0 - 2.4
	2.5 - 2.9
	3.0 - 3.4
	3.5 - 3.9
	4.0 - 4.4
	4.5 - 5.0

Scale 1 (Disagree strongly) - 5 (Agree strongly)

Factors contributing to a successful marriage

Scale o (Not at all important) - 1 (Very important)

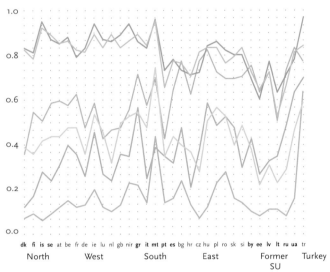

dk fi is se at be fr de ie lu nl gb nir gr it mt pt es bg hr cz hu pl ro sk si by ee lv lt ru ua tr

| North | West | South | East | Former SU | Turkey |

— Fidelity
— Personal bond
— Pair orientation
— Children
— Material conditions
— Cultural homogeneity

In Europe, marriage is regarded as an interpersonal relationship, and less so as an institution. This may be concluded from the figure displaying the factors that contribute to a successful marriage. Europeans judge the quality of a marriage predominantly by affective qualities such as faithfulness and a strong personal bond, i.e. affection, mutual respect and appreciation, understanding and tolerance. And with the exception of Turkey, material conditions such as good housing and an adequate income, cultural homogeneity and pair orientation (the opportunity to live as a pair) are considered of minor importance. In the East the presence of children seems quite important for a successful marriage unlike in the west where other factors seem to be more important for the establishment of a successful marriage.

Success factors for marriage according to age

The importance of factors contributing to a successful marriage in age groups.
Scale o (Not at all important) - 1 (Very important)

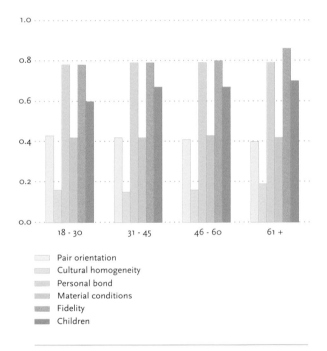

| 18 - 30 | 31 - 45 | 46 - 60 | 61 + |

Pair orientation
Cultural homogeneity
Personal bond
Material conditions
Fidelity
Children

Agreement with the statement that a marriage or a long-term stable relationship is necessary to be happy according to civil status

Scale 1 (Disagree strongly) - 5 (Agree strongly)

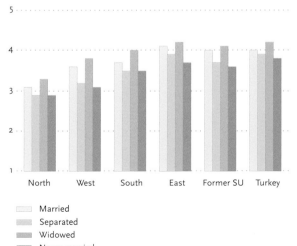

| North | West | South | East | Former SU | Turkey |

Married
Separated
Widowed
Never married

"Whereas we used to find a partner of the same religious background and social origin, we now find a spouse of the same educational level."

Wilfred Uunk
Assistant Professor
of Social Cultural Sciences

Dr. Wilfred Uunk is an assistant professor of Social Cultural Sciences at Tilburg University, the Netherlands.
Contact: w.uunk@uvt.nl.

"Marriage is not outdated and never will be. Everybody wants a mate, a partner for life. Partnership is a general goal in life, a kind of biological invariable, because a he or she brings love, happiness and the possibility of offspring. Although the concept of marriage is alive and well, the institution of marriage has evolved over the past few decades. People choose their partner on different grounds than they did fifty years ago, and they have different, notably higher, expectations of the relationship. People also tend to marry later in life or not at all. This delay in marriage has to do with both economic and cultural factors. Increased wealth of households and greater female participation in the workforce have weakened the economic necessity for the opposite sexes to pool resources and to marry early. This may be a reason why the mean age of a first marriage is lower in the poorer Southern European countries than in the richer Northern European countries. It is obviously not a sufficient reason. Italians, for example, deviate by rather high mean ages of first marriages. Italians marry late not because of economic security, but because of economic insecurity as they are confronted with high youth employment, and high education and housing costs. Cultural factors are a second set of factors in explaining variations in age of marriage. Due to the process of secularization and individualization people attach weaker value to the institution of marriage. Another important cultural factor contributing to postponement of marriage is the general rise in educational level. Due to this European-wide trend, people wait longer to enter wedlock. This has both to do with the time education takes, the type of partner market one finds oneself in (smaller marriage market during university studies), the insight on gains on marriage during education, and the normative expectations of family, friends and fellow students.

Romance
In our contemporary European societies with their ideals of romantic love, marriage selection seems socially chaotic and predominantly a matter of personal taste. Anybody can marry anybody. Perhaps that is true, but is this the reality? However irrational men and women may be during early stages of love, when long-lived bonds between people are considered the love market turns out to be far from socially blind. But whereas we once found a partner of the same religious background and social origin, we now find a spouse of the same educational level.

A large part of this trend can be explained by the laws of probability. Whereas young adults used to meet each other at the catholic or protestant evening dances - depending on their religious affiliation, they now meet most of their peers during college or university. I do not say romance does not exist, but if a boy meets ten girls of his educational level and one above or below, the chances of falling in love with a girl of his own level are definitely higher. Education acts as a first filter, replacing social origin and religion as a marker of one's cultural and economic resources, but also occurs because people 'profit' from such a marriage more than from an educationally mixed marriage. Similarly educated partners generally have more in common than educationally heterogeneous people.

It is to be noted that social factors cannot explain all patterns in mate selection. Partners' ages at marriage, for example, pose a problem for social scientists. Throughout history and throughout the world, men are a few years older than their spouses. This universal finding points to the role played by biology. In ancient times, women preferred older men as they had proven their providing or hunting capacities; men chose younger, healthier women with the prospect of having more children. It is striking in our modern times this age-specific pattern still exists.

An interesting question is, of course, if an equal level of education is a better or more solid basis for marriage, than a shared religion or a shared social status by the spouses' fathers.

This is not an easy topic to research. Comparing today's divorce rates with those of fifty years ago is complex, as people have far higher expectations of marriage today, and divorce has become far more common. A study by the Dutch social scientist Jacques Janssen showed that the risk of divorce in the Netherlands only increases when the bride is better educated than the groom, not when the man is more highly educated than his wife. The odds of divorce rise by twenty percent."

Unconditional love

Percentage of people who agree with the
statement "Regardless of what the qualities
and faults of one's parents are, one must
always love and respect them"

- < 50 %
- 50 - 59 %
- 60 - 69 %
- 70 - 79 %
- 80 - 89 %
- 90 - 100 %

Sacrifice and unconditional love

A B

- Sacrifice
- No sacrifice
- Neutral

Europeans were asked if parents should
make personal sacrifices for their children
ánd if children should show unconditional
love for their parents. The expectation being
that these two views would show some
correlation: someone who believes that
children should show unconditional love for
one's parents is expected to also underline
the view that parents on their account should
be prepared to make sacrifices. One can
see it as a kind of moral reciprocity: you
cannot expect unconditional loyalty from your
children when you do not show it yourself.

And indeed this correlation was found. Pie A,
on the left, shows the support for the opinion
that it is a parents' duty to do their best for
their children even at the expense of their
own well-being for those Europeans who find
that children should show unconditional love
and respect for their parents. Almost three
quarters endorse the reciprocal view.
Pie B shows the opinion about the statement
that parents should be prepared to make
sacrifices for those Europeans who do not
agree that children should always show
unconditional love. It is evident that parents

who don't expect unconditional love from
their children, are less of the opinion
that parents should be prepared to make
sacrifices at the expense of their own well-
being. Yet, a (small) majority still underlines
this vision. Apparently, a majority of
Europeans feels that parents should always
do their utmost best for their children, no
matter what.

A considerable majority (circa 70%) of Europeans expect children to have unconditional love for and faith in parents; an equal percentage say parents should be prepared to sacrifice their well-being for their children

Percentage of people who tend to agree with the statement "Parents' duty is to do their best for their children even at the expense of their own well-being"

< 50 %
50 - 59 %
60 - 69 %
70 - 79 %
80 - 89 %
90 - 100 %

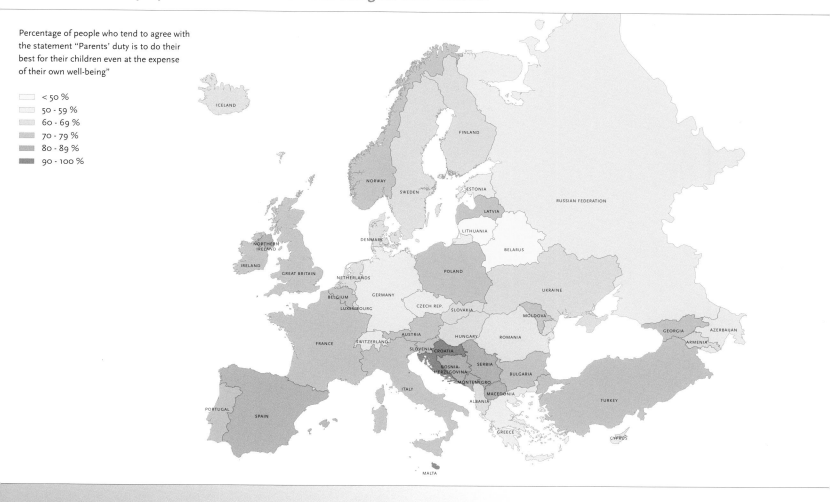

Sweden - Russia:
Individualized versus traditional parent-child relationships

Child rearing has become less a process of disciplinary supervision and more a question of personal attention to the emotional and social aspects of a child's development.
As a consequence, the distance between parent and child has been significantly reduced.
The status of the child within the family unit as well as in society has greatly increased over the past decades, although within the family this status may vary considerably.
This development is part of an ongoing process of individualization, which has obviously effected the parent-child relationship. Within Europe there are large differences in parent-child relationships. In the western part of Europe a democratic or individualized style of parenting ('mild control, high warmth') is customary. Democratic parent-child relationships appear when parents give their children choices and spend time discussing with their children the reasons behind the rules they make. Sweden seems a clear example in this respect. The traditional parent-child relationship exists when parents are strict, dictating many rules and expecting these rules to be obeyed without explanation. This style of parenting is called authoritarian ('high control, low warmth') when children are not allowed to ask questions or to have their own opinions, or authoritative ('high control, high warmth') when parents communicate their expectations and show reason and flexibility. Russia is a prime example of traditional parent-child relations.

Working mother or housewife

Incompatible expectations

The survey of the European Values Studies includes several questions about the appropriate role of women (see also page 39), for example: Do women prefer a home and children? Should they contribute to the household income? Are pre-school children likely to suffer when their mothers work? On the basis of the results, one may conclude that Europeans are not against the concept of working mothers. More than 60% agree with the statement 'A job is alright but what most women really want is a home and children'.

There also appear some clear inconsistencies in people's views on working women. For example, the majority of Europeans agree with both the statement that 'A pre-school kid is likely to suffer when his or her mother works' and with the (almost incompatible) statement that 'A working mother can establish just as warm and secure a relationship with her children as a mother who does not work'. In Greece, 78% agree with the first statement, 76% with the second. In the Ukraine, these numbers are 73% and 83%, respectively.

Another seeming inconsistency is found when people are asked if both the husband and wife should contribute to the household income. 81% of the Italians expect the wife to provide an income for the family, however the same high percentage underlines the saying that a pre-school kid is likely to suffer when his or her mother works. Obviously, Italian women cannot fulfil both societal 'demands'; they are faced with incompatible expectations. And surprisingly, the two European peoples who least subscribe to the view that a job is alright but what most women really want is a home and children, also the least expect women to contribute to the household income. Another apparent inconsistency.

Opinions on working mothers according to gender
Scale 1 (Strongly disagree) - 4 (Strongly agree)

Agreement with the statements:
a A working mother can establish just as warm and secure a relationship with her children as a mother who does not work
b Being a housewife is just as fulfilling as working for pay
c Both the husband and wife should contribute to household income

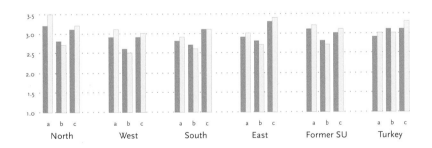

Opinions on working mothers according to level of education
Scale 1 (Strongly disagree) - 4 (Strongly agree)

Agreement with the statements:
a A working mother can establish just as warm and secure a relationship with her children as a mother who does not work
b Being a housewife is just as fulfilling as working for pay
c Both the husband and wife should contribute to household income

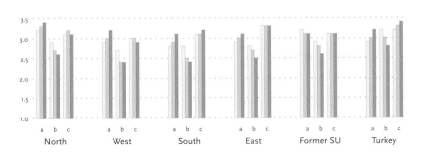

70% of Italians think that a pre-school child is likely to suffer if his or her mother works, yet 65% also agree with the statement that a working mother can establish just as warm and secure a relationship with her children as a mother who does work

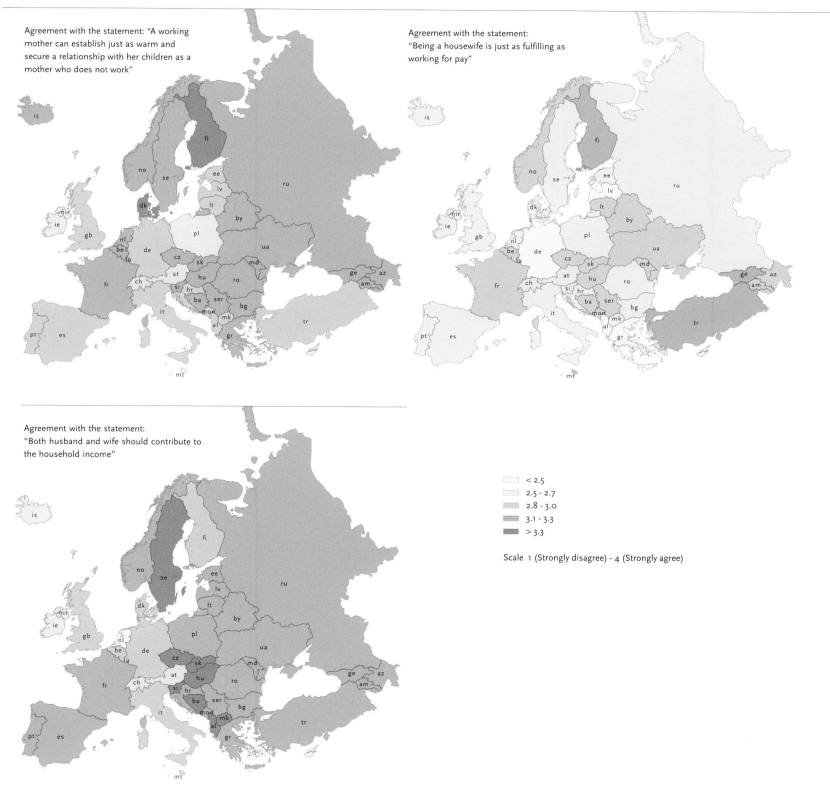

Agreement with the statement: "A working mother can establish just as warm and secure a relationship with her children as a mother who does not work"

Agreement with the statement: "Being a housewife is just as fulfilling as working for pay"

Agreement with the statement: "Both husband and wife should contribute to the household income"

	< 2.5
	2.5 - 2.7
	2.8 - 3.0
	3.1 - 3.3
	> 3.3

Scale 1 (Strongly disagree) - 4 (Strongly agree)

Transmission of values

Good old manners

What values do Europeans want to teach their children? An important question, because one may expect that people tend to pass on those values that they regard of the highest importance. In the European Values Studies survey people could select five qualities from a list of eleven that they would encourage children to learn at home. These included traditional values such as hard work, good manners, obedience and good faith, which have always been emphasized in authoritarian parenting and by religious institutions. Also more modern qualities were on the list, for example, independence, imagination, tolerance and determination.

These are important tools for living in a highly individualized modern society.
Four of the eleven values are far more popular than the others, these are: responsibility, good manners, tolerance and respect for other people and hard work. They form an interesting mix of traditional and modern values. Tolerance and respect are prototypes of (post)modern values, good manners and hard work are traditional values, responsibility has also been claimed by modernists, however it can also be seen as a classical quality, although perhaps with a different meaning. The traditional quality, hard work, has clearly more support in Eastern Europe than in

the Western and Northern regions following the lines of modernization. However, another explanation can be that it reflects a heritage of the socialist and communist doctrine.
The other traditional value, good manners, is popular throughout Europe, indicating that also the modern, individualizing society desires politeness of its citizens. Conclusion: good old manners are timeless.

Percentage of people who want to encourage their children to learn this value

- 0 - 12.4 %
- 12.5 - 24.9 %
- 25.0 - 37.4 %
- 37.5 - 49.9 %
- 50.0 - 62.4 %
- 62.5 - 74.9 %
- 75.0 - 87.4 %
- 87.5 - 100 %

The importance of the various values that Europeans want to encourage to teach their children at home

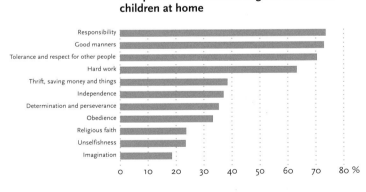

Obedience

Responsibility, good manners, tolerance and respect are by far the most
important values that Europeans want to pass on to their children;
religious faith, unselfishness and obedience are not half as important

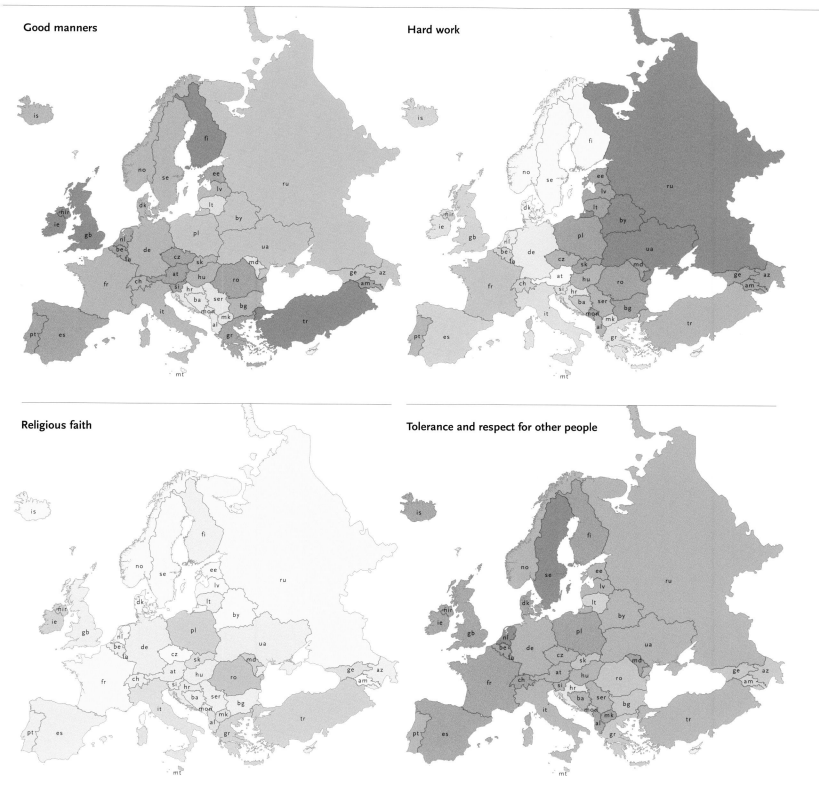

Good manners

Hard work

Religious faith

Tolerance and respect for other people

(Dis)agreement between generations

All parents wish to see their children hold values that they have in high regard, i.e. their own values. However, probably to the great disappointment of many parents, most academic studies have found only moderate, sometimes even not statistically significant, correlations between the values of parents and their children. For example, the parents of student activists were not more politically active than the parents of non-active students.

Acquiring a personal value set is a complex process that takes place in a context much more encompassing than the nuclear family. Friends, the peer group, the neighbourhood, the school, the nation at large, all play a part in forming a child. Therefore it is highly unlikely that children will grow up in a world that contains only one set of values, that reflect that of their parents.

Moreover, these 'other' value sets may run counter to those that parents wish to see their children to hold. Parents may therefore try to keep their children away from 'bad' influences as long as possible ('cocooning') or may teach their children to ignore these influences: "They are just ignorant, jealous, badly brought up, etc.". Another strategy that parents use is internalization, the process in which a moral point of view becomes a part of a natural order, a concept of the self, which is unthinkable to depart from. For example, after having said "Say please" to their child many times, parents move on to the phrase "What is the magic word?". If politeness has truly become internalized this question is no longer needed and becomes a rhetorical one.

Percentage of people who want to encourage their children to learn this value

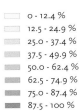

- 0 - 12.4 %
- 12.5 - 24.9 %
- 25.0 - 37.4 %
- 37.5 - 49.9 %
- 50.0 - 62.4 %
- 62.5 - 74.9 %
- 75.0 - 87.4 %
- 87.5 - 100 %

Independence

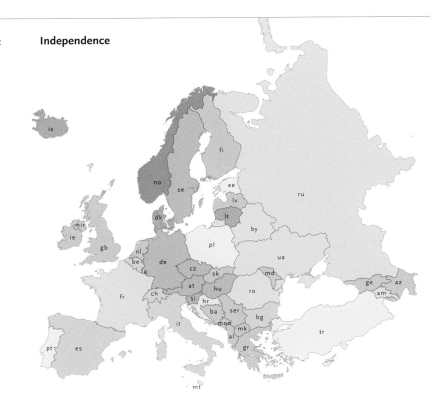

Thrift, saving money and things

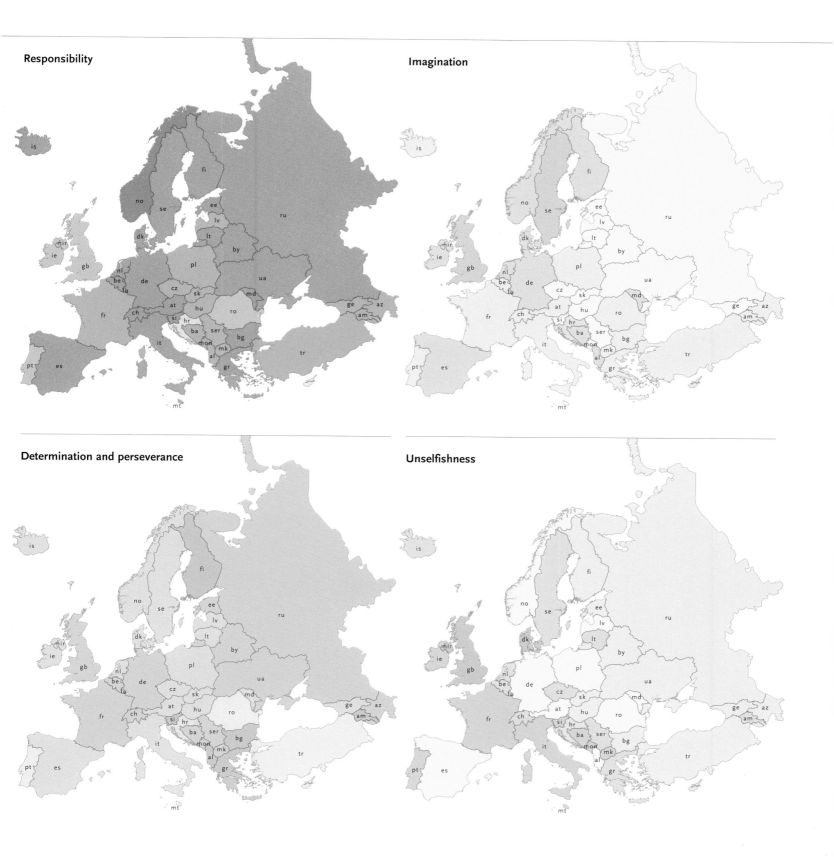

Responsibility

Imagination

Determination and perseverance

Unselfishness

BANK STATION

↓ Central line
↓ District and Circle lines
↓ Northern line
↓ Waterloo & City line
↓ Docklands trains
↓ Public subway
  Toilets

Work

Work, for some it is a dire necessity, for others just pursuing a virtuous vocation. For all, however, a time-consuming event: forty hours a week for forty years. It is therefore no surprise that work is characterized as 'very important' by 70% of all Europeans. And, whereas in the Middle Ages work meant hard, physical labour on the land, today, many have the possibility to choose an occupation that suits them. This makes work a central feature in people's lives.

Europe's labour force consists of 250 million people who work on average 40 hours a week with about 25 days leave a year. About half of the Europeans are active in the service sector; only about 10% work in agriculture and the remainder in industry. However, the variation amongst the European countries is large. In the Northern and Western parts less than 5% of the working population is involved in agriculture, whereas the economies of Moldova, Turkey and Romania still have a dominant agrarian character. The Czech, Slovak and - to a lesser extent - the German and Austrian economies may be categorised as industrial. Most countries can be best described as service economies. Women account for 40% of the European workforce and their participation is rising. Families in which the man is the

only breadwinner are becoming scarce. The variation in job participation by women amongst European countries is again large. In the Netherlands the majority of women who work do so on a part-time basis (this trend is also visible in the male workforce) to be able to combine family and working life. In Scandinavian countries full time jobs are the custom for both men and women; the state provides the necessary childcare. In the countries formerly belonging to the Soviet Union the participation of women in the workforce is the highest. The communists encouraged equality of women in the professional sphere and today work is often an economic necessity for both sexes. Participation of women is the lowest in southern European countries like Greece, Italy, Spain and Turkey.

Curse or blessing

Philosopher Hannah Arendt (1906-1975) made the distinction between 'work' and 'labour'. The term 'Work' has a positive overtone: performing meaningful, creative activities, which allow for personal development. 'Labour' has a negative connotation: it refers to aggravating, dulling, routine work, which affects one's well-being. From the European Values Studies one can conclude that most Europeans view their job as 'work'; only the people in Belarus on average qualify their job as dissatisfying.

To the Greeks and Romans labour meant slavery; those wealthy enough to afford slaves could avoid having to labour. The early Christians considered labour as a punishment: a penalty for the 'original sin' (Genesis 3:19 "in the sweat of thy face shalt thou

Unemployment rate 2003

- 0.0 - 3.9 %
- 4.0 - 6.9 %
- 7.0 - 9.9 %
- 10.0 - 12.9 %
- ≥ 13.0 %

Source: Economic Survey of Europe, 2004 No.1

eat bread"). It was not until the reformation and especially Martin Luther and John Calvin that not only work, but also labour, received a more positive connotation. To them labour was a vocation. One should not waste the talents given by God. The virtues and duties of the reformation have rooted in Europe's societies. Today, 63% of Europeans agree with the statement 'people who don't work turn lazy' and 62% endorse the declaration 'work is a duty towards society'. But when one colours today's Europe according to a work ethos (see page 55) no religious patterns are found. Work simply appears to be an economic necessity; the lower the income and wealth, the higher the work ethos. Also, surprisingly, a high work ethos doesn't lead to job satisfaction (see page 53). The inhabitants of the wealthier

European countries are more satisfied with their jobs than those with a lower income. Apparently, wealth allows people to make their work more pleasant.
Most remarkable is perhaps the difference in job satisfaction between the (few) farmers in Western and Northern Europe and the (many) farmers in the Eastern part and Turkey. Farming in Northern and Western Europe is highly satisfying, whereas farming in the East is an unsatisfying occupation.

Self-development
A contemporary discussion in sociology centres on people's work orientation. Ronald Inglehart, Professor of Political Sciences at the University of Michigan started the debate in his book *Modernization and Postmodernization: Cultural,*

Economic and Political Change in 43 Societies (1997). He discerns expressive and instrumental work orientations. In a post-modern society that guarantees welfare and well-being, the working man and woman will value expressive work qualities more than instrumental ones, argues Inglehart. Work has become a domain in which people can develop, nurture, and cultivate themselves; the post-modern worker wants an interesting job that is useful for society and that meets one's abilities. For the time being however, Inglehart's hypothesis is not supported by the European Values Studies (see page 53). Good pay is the number one valued job aspect in all European countries in all generations. The European Union depends on the highly motivated, highly creative post-modern worker to launch

Europe into the global economy and the average European's focus on salary may come as a disappointment. Even the post-modern worker desires proper monetary compensation for his or her work.

Importance of work

The end of jobs

Industrialization, automation and later computerization, led many utopians to predict a future in which work is no longer necessary, or at least, no major activity in our lives. The French economist Jean Fourastié, for instance, forecasted in 1965 a sharp decline in labour activities once consumption would be satisfied. In 1985, the German social scientist Claus Offe concluded that other activities gained importance at the cost of labour. And in 1994, the well-known author of management books William Bridges, published an article in the business magazine Fortune titled 'The end of jobs'. Jobs would not fit in the post-industrial society, according to the management advisor.

However, jobs have not vanished, at least not yet. According to the European Values Studies and many other sources, work has retained its importance in contemporary society. What has changed dramatically is the type of jobs we have. People are no longer employed in the industrial sector, but in the service sector. Work has changed because of large-scale structural and cultural developments. The fraction of Europeans however, that consider work not important is with less than 9% almost negligible, and nearly 60% of all Europeans consider work to be very important. Work ranks above friends, religion and leisure time in importance, only giving precedence to family.

Work versus leisure time
Importance of work – Importance of leisure time (%)

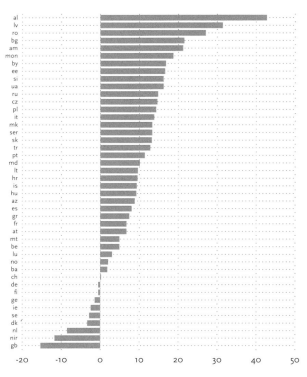

The European Values Studies inquired both after the importance of work and leisure time. Here is presented the percentage considering their job 'very or rather important' minus the percentage considering leisure time 'very or rather important'. In this way countries are ordered according to their appreciation for work versus leisure time.

Importance of work for the (not) employed

Very important
Quite important
Not important
Not at all important

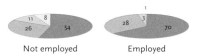

Not employed   Employed

Importance of work according to age

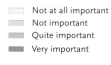

Not at all important
Not important
Quite important
Very important

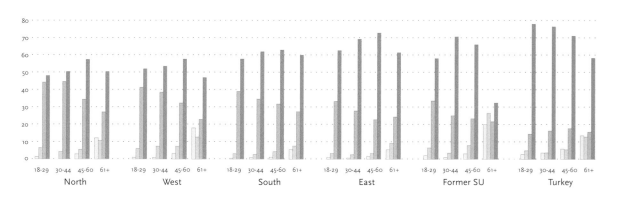

North   West   South   East   Former SU   Turkey

82% of the Albanians consider their work very important, the highest rate in Europe; with a score of 39% the inhabitants of Denmark seem the least attached to their job

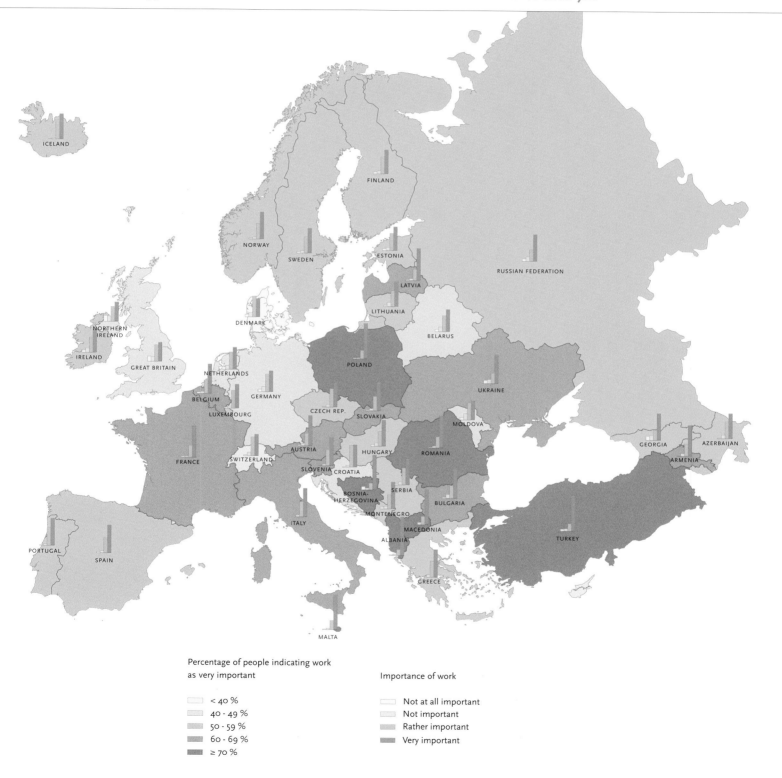

Percentage of people indicating work as very important

- ⬜ < 40 %
- ⬜ 40 - 49 %
- ⬜ 50 - 59 %
- ⬜ 60 - 69 %
- ⬛ ≥ 70 %

Importance of work

- ⬜ Not at all important
- ⬜ Not important
- ⬜ Rather important
- ⬛ Very important

Importance of work qualities

Importance of expressive work qualities

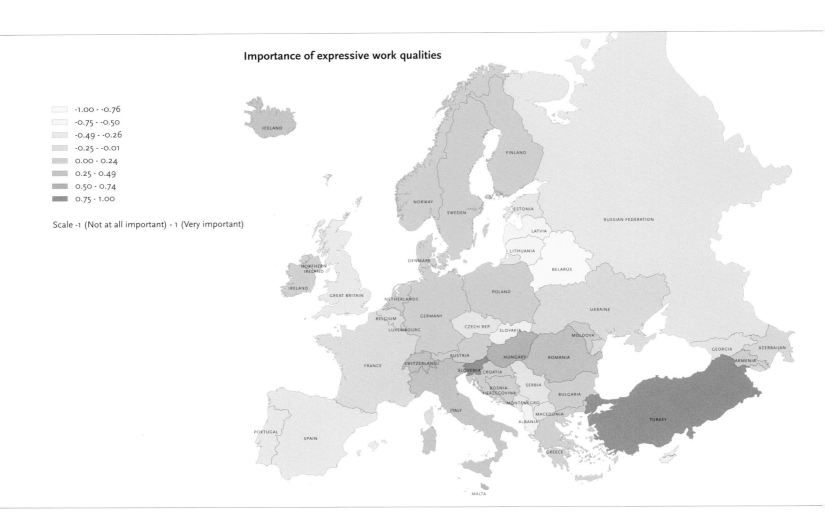

☐	-1.00 - -0.76
☐	-0.75 - -0.50
☐	-0.49 - -0.26
▨	-0.25 - -0.01
▨	0.00 - 0.24
▨	0.25 - 0.49
▨	0.50 - 0.74
▨	0.75 - 1.00

Scale -1 (Not at all important) - 1 (Very important)

Good pay

According to post-modernisation theories, today's worker wants an interesting job that is useful for society and that meets his or hers abilities. Good pay, job security and other instrumental job aspects are less important to the post-modern worker. Work is primarily seen as the life domain in which people can develop, nurture and cultivate themselves.
Concluding from the data of the European Values Study, the European worker does not fit this picture of the post-modern employee. On the contrary, Europeans considers good pay and good job security the most important job aspects (see page 52). Expressive job aspects only rank in 3rd to 7th position, in the following order: pleasant people to work with, a job that meets one's abilities, a job that is interesting, and a job in which one can achieve something.
However, the intra-country differences are large, causing the balance to tip slightly in favour of expressive work values in the Northern and Western part of Europe, and in favour of instrumental work values in the other parts. But even a majority of the Danes, who score lowest on instrumental values, think good pay and job security are valuable assets. Turkey is a remarkable exception in all respects. The Turks seem to value all job aspects very highly; perhaps this is a result of their altogether very high dedication to work: 75 percent of the Turks consider work very important. Yet, 91 percent of the Turks appreciate low pressure on the job, which is the highest in Europe. Here, the Danes score lowest; only 40 percent considers work very important in their lives. Some other interesting 'lows': only 32 percent of the Latvians find 'pleasant people to work with' an important job aspect; only 17 percent of the Danish find 'chances for promotion' an important job aspect; only 22 percent of the Russians find 'a job useful for society' an important job aspect and only 23 percent of the Slovaks find 'meeting people' important in their job.

Turkish people value instrumental work qualities such as good pay and job security as highly as expressive work qualities such as interesting and respected work

Importance of instrumental work qualities

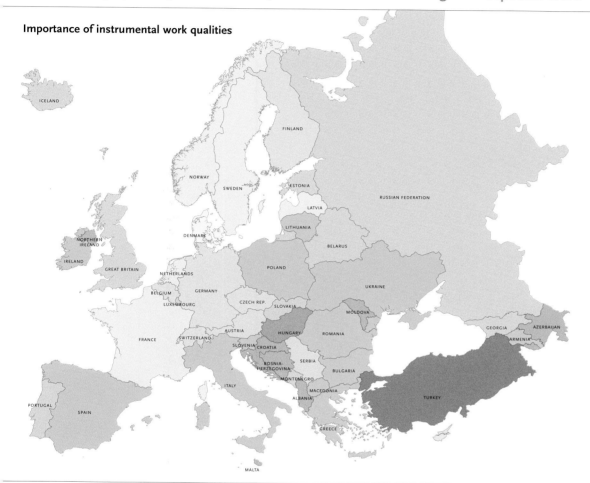

A classical distinction in work values is the one between instrumental (also named extrinsic) and expressive (or intrinsic) work qualities. Expressive work qualities concern non-material or post material job characteristics such as personal development, achievement and autonomy. People who value such expressive work values see work as a means of utilizing their capacities, whereas people who value instrumental work qualities see work primarily as a means to achieve goals outside their work. For these people the income and the securities offered by work are most important.

Here, the importance of expressive and instrumental work qualities was calculated for each European country by combining scores on various job aspects. For expressive work important qualities are: freedom to take initiative, job responsibility, personal sense of achievement, utilization of one's skill, interest of job, social environment, contribution to society, professional respect, professional mobility and pleasant social environment. The importance of instrumental work qualities is based on the appreciation of reasonable hours, generous holidays, good pay, relaxed work environment, job security, possibility for promotion and professional respect.

Importance of work qualities by gender

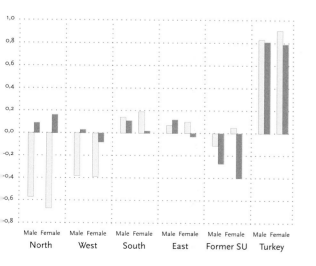

Importance of work qualities for the (not) employed

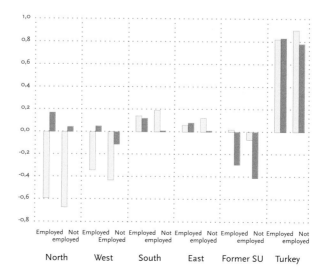

Instrumental work qualities important

Expressive work qualities important

Scale -1 (Not at all important) - 1 (Very important)

Expressive versus instrumental work qualities

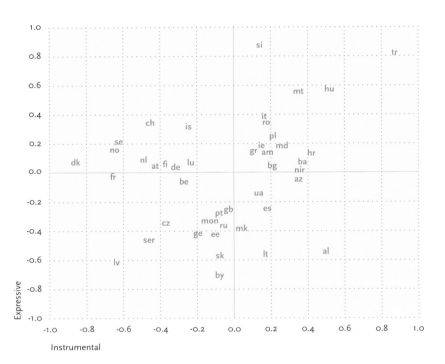

Instrumental

Expressive

Here the score of each country on work qualities is given in an expressive-instrumental work qualities dimension. Countries are presented by their abbreviations. According to classical (post)-modernization theory, post-modern societies will be found in the upper-left quadrant. Inhabitants of post-modern societies are expected to value expressive work qualities highly; instrumental values are no longer important as an income is 'guaranteed' by the welfare state.

The importance of an interesting job

Percentage of people who find having an interesting job is important

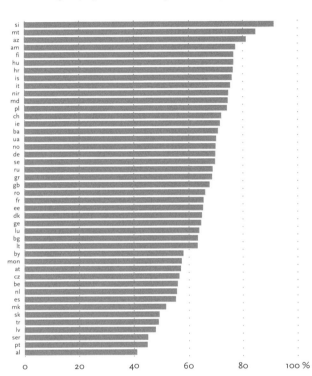

Important job aspects

Percentage of Europeans who indicate the job aspect as important

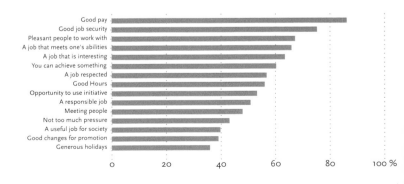

"The idea that the post-modern worker values self-development higher than job-security and good pay is somewhat naive"

Peter Ester
Professor of Sociology

Prof. Dr. Peter Ester is a professor of Sociology at Tilburg University, the Netherlands, Director of OSA, Institute for Labour Studies in Tilburg and 2003-2005 visiting professor at ZUMA, Center for Survey Research and Methodology, Mannheim, Germany

"For Europeans the meaning of work has changed substantially in the last few decades. Work has become far more than just a necessity that provides an income. It is also a way to develop one's talents and employability, to add to society's progress, to challenge one's intellect and to achieve social standing and respect. At least, this is true for those Europeans who live in a welfare state and can rely on a solid social security system. In academic terms we say that in the knowledge-based economy post-modern or expressive work qualities have gained in importance in addition to conventional or instrumental work qualities such as good hours and a good salary.

As a result of the rise of post-modern values the traditional borders between work and other life-domains such as family, education and leisure fade away. One reads a management book for fun, goes jogging with colleagues and doesn't turn off the mobile phone after office hours. The labour market anticipated this development by becoming 'transitional': people are enabled to make smooth and pro-active transitions to, on, and from work in order to optimize the combination of work, care, study and 'free time'. Working hours become flexible, employees may save up time for a holiday and companies promote having a computer at home. This development also reflects the current individualization in society: the personal life course becomes increasingly diversified and subject to personal values, choices and preferences.

Several sociologists assume that the post-modern worker exchanges instrumental work qualities for expressive work qualities: an interesting job would become more valuable than a secure one. This hypothesis is somewhat, if not quite naive. Job security is and will remain highly valued by youngsters. They are at the start of their career and life course; they want to marry, buy a house and have children, all of which require a stable and solid income. Modern life may provide much freedom, but the many choices also bring along larger responsibilities. Making a choice in education today has many consequences for your future career. It is therefore not surprising that good pay is still the highest job-value for Europeans, closely followed by job security. Studies do prove that younger people value expressive work qualities more than elderly: an interesting and challenging job is high on their agenda. However, the rise of expressive qualities doesn't result in less appreciation for the traditional instrumental values. Expressive work qualities are an addition to the traditional values, not a replacement.

Burnout

Nowadays work is only matched, in importance, by family. Friends, religion and leisure time are (relatively) considered less important. However, all life domains are qualified by a majority, as 'important'. But all these domains compete in time allocation. As a consequence the modern European worker experiences feelings of pressure. He or she is not only expected to be a flexible and a knowledgeable employee with a keen eye for maintaining and renewing core skills. He or she is also obliged to be a good, caring parent and partner, maintaining a respectable relational network and participating in varied and distinct leisure activities.

It is not only society that expects people to excel in all life domains; we desire it too! We want that shining career, we want to be a loving parent, look perfect, read the latest best-seller and attend the latest concert. Post-modern values are becoming internalized. From a social point of view this is a highly interesting development: how do people fill in their life in between all these competing values? Without a doubt it leads to a far more personalized and varied life course. However, it also has a dark side. Whereas only two decades ago we became familiar with the term mid-life crisis, today it is not uncommon to experience a first 'burnout' in your late twenties. When our personal ambitions in work and life are high a disillusion is always near."

Job satisfaction

Job satisfaction versus freedom of decision making

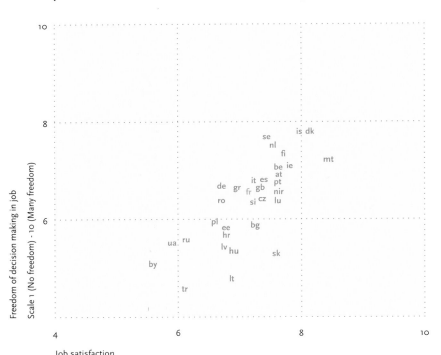

Freedom of decision making in job
Scale 1 (No freedom) - 10 (Many freedom)

Job satisfaction
Scale 1 (Very dissatisfied) - 10 (Highly satisfied)

In the 1960s and 1970s, theories were put forward that a feeling of control over one's work improves job satisfaction (and performance). Indeed studies since then appear to be consistent in that high levels of worker control are associated with high levels of job satisfaction and low levels of stress (anxiety, psychological distress, burnout, irritability and even alcohol consumption). In a longitudinally study among London-based civil servants, low levels of job control were predictive of coronary heart disease. As can be seen in this graph, there is a strong link between job satisfaction and freedom of decision making. In sociology the term 'locus of control' is often used for freedom of decision making. Locus of control refers to a person's beliefs about the sources of control over life. Individuals with low levels of perceived control (externals) believe outside forces, fate, or other people determine what happens to them, while people who have high levels of perceived control (internals) believe they are in control themselves.

Job satisfaction according to type of profession
The percentage of satisfied minus the percentage of unsatisfied people, by type of profession

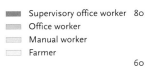

- Supervisory office worker
- Office worker
- Manual worker
- Farmer

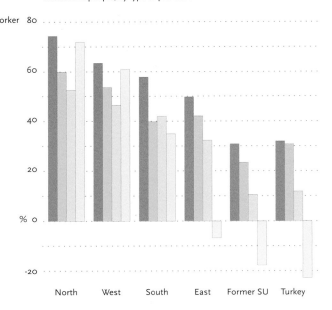

Job satisfaction by gender

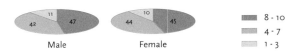

Male   Female

- 8 - 10
- 4 - 7
- 1 - 3

Scale 1 (Not at all satisfied) - 10 (Very satisfied)

On a scale of 1-10 the French rate their job a 7;
only the people in Belarus qualify their jobs as dissatisfying: 5.5;
the Maltese are by far the most satisfied: they rate their job an 8.4

< 6
6.0 - 6.4
6.5 - 6.9
7.0 - 7.4
7.5 - 7.9
≥ 8.0

Scale 1 (Not at all satisfied) - 10 (Very satisfied)

Work ethos

Economic success and work ethos

Work ethos or work ethic is a cultural norm that places a positive moral value on doing a good job. It is based on the belief that work has an intrinsic value.
In the Western world job ethos is a relatively new concept. It was not until the Protestant Reformation in the 16th century that physical labour became culturally acceptable for all persons, even the wealthy (see also Work ethos in Germany, page 55).
The Protestant work ethic is believed to be one of the driving forces behind the economic prosperity of the USA and Europe. As is the Confucian moral behind the economic successes of the Asian 'dragons' such as Japan, Taiwan and Hong Kong. Confucius propagated diligence and thrift. There are, however, marked differences between the Protestant and Confucian (work) ethic. The most manifest difference is that Protestant ethic advocates individualism, while Confucius stresses the collective nature of society.
The data of the European Values Study and the World Values Survey, show that today's Europe has a higher work ethos than Japan or the USA. Respectively, 62, 61 and 58 percent of the Europeans, Japanese and Americans agree with the statement 'Work is a duty towards society'. For the statement 'It's humiliating to receive money without having to work for it', these numbers are 56, 43 and 37 percent. The new rising economies show a considerably higher work ethos. Both in India and China the support for these statements are above 80 percent.

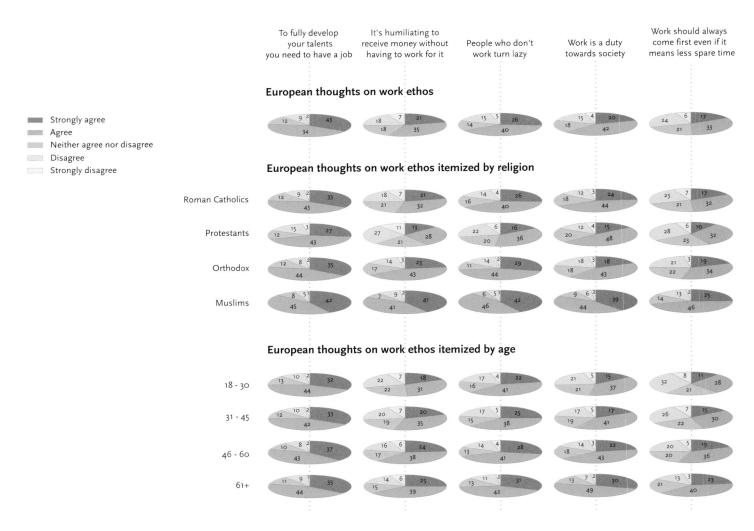

Strongly agree
Agree
Neither agree nor disagree
Disagree
Strongly disagree

To fully develop your talents you need to have a job

It's humiliating to receive money without having to work for it

People who don't work turn lazy

Work is a duty towards society

Work should always come first even if it means less spare time

European thoughts on work ethos

European thoughts on work ethos itemized by religion

Roman Catholics

Protestants

Orthodox

Muslims

European thoughts on work ethos itemized by age

18 - 30

31 - 45

46 - 60

61+

63% of the Europeans agree with the statement 'people who don't work turn lazy'

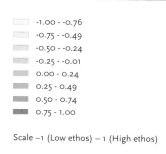

-1.00 - -0.76
-0.75 - -0.49
-0.50 - -0.24
-0.25 - -0.01
0.00 - 0.24
0.25 - 0.49
0.50 - 0.74
0.75 - 1.00

Scale −1 (Low ethos) − 1 (High ethos)

Work ethos or work ethic represents the degree to which individuals place work at or near the center of their lives. Persons with a strong work ethic regard hard work as intrinsically good and as almost a moral duty. In contrast, they regard leisure somewhat suspiciously because of its potential to harm both persons and society as a whole.

The level of work ethos for each European country can be calculated using the inhabitants opinions about the following five statements: (1) To fully develop your talents, you need to have a job, (2) It is humiliating to receive money without having to work for it, (3) People who don't work, turn lazy, (4) Work is a duty towards society, (5) Work should always come first, even if it means less spare time.

-1.00 - -0.76
-0.75 - -0.49
-0.50 - -0.24
-0.25 - -0.01
0.00 - 0.24
0.25 - 0.49
0.50 - 0.74
0.75 - 1.00

Scale −1 (Low ethos) − 1 (High ethos)

Work ethos in Germany

Germany is one of the few European countries in which Protestants and Catholics are more or less evenly represented. Protestantism is the dominant religion in the northern part; Catholicism in the southern part. One of the leading scholars in and founders of modern sociology, Max Weber (1864-1920) argued that Protestant societies had a special work ethos which played an important role in the development of Capitalism in western societies. Analyses of the European Values Study cannot substantiate this idea. Today, work ethic is not (or no longer) associated with Protestantism, as is exemplified by the work ethos in Germany. For much of the ancient history of the human race, work has been hard and degrading. Working hard - in the absence of compulsion - was definitely not the norm for Hebrew, classical, or medieval cultures. This changed during the reformation in the 16th century, when John Calvin and Martin Luther introduced new theological doctrines. To the Protestants all work, however menial, had inherent dignity and value. In fact, diligence in the performance of work was seen as perhaps the highest form of Christian obedience. Physical labour became culturally acceptable for all persons, even the wealthy.

Max Weber called this ethos the Protestant Work Ethic (PWE). According to Weber Protestants are more work-oriented than non-protestants.

He did not argue that a non-protestant society cannot produce "the spirit of capitalism", rather he emphasized the fact that Catholicism and Islam had not developed such a spirit in their history.

Obedience to one's superior

Blind obedience

Obedience seems quite inconsistent with (post-)modern ideals such as individualization, autonomy, independence, and anti-authoritarianism. Yet, obedience can be extremely functional in the workplace, particularly in emergencies and high-stress situations. For example, having someone in command on battle grounds or in a surgery is essential to ensure success. However, the mentality of 'I was only obeying orders' has proven incredibly harmful to humanity throughout history. In modern management,

obedience, authoritarian leadership and power are banned from the vocabulary of the workplace. It has become evident that enterprises organised along strict authoritarian lines meet many problems especially now that tasks are becoming more and more complex. When orders are followed immediately without any questioning, wrong orders and mistakes are not corrected. People within authoritarian ruled firms tend to avoid making decisions as they are under constant fear and stress of losing their job because of a mistake. Often blame

for mistakes is passed on to others, creating an atmosphere of distrust. Furthermore, employees experience little room for showing their talents and they are not likely to enjoy the success of their company as their own. While a fear-based management style can accomplish impressive short-term results, the long-term consequences can be devastating. In modern management, leadership and authority are associated with more positive, individual assets like good communication skills, an excellent reputation, knowledge

and intelligence, flexibility, and high tolerance for conflict. Modern management is all about coaching, supporting, directing, and inspiring people. However, authority in the form of formal authority is widely accepted. People in higher positions are far more likely to be obeyed without questioning than lower staff or fellow workers. That is, when trust within a company is high. In that case, employees are confident that those in charge have earned their position on the basis of their skills and talents.

Obedience by job type

Follow instructions
Must be convinced first
Depends

Self employed • Supervising employees • Non-supervising employees

Obedience by gender

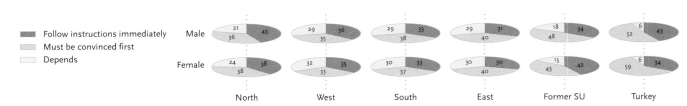

Follow instructions immediately
Must be convinced first
Depends

Male • Female

North • West • South • East • Former SU • Turkey

62% of Armenians needs to be convinced first before following their superior's instructions; 60% of Norwegians follow instructions immediately

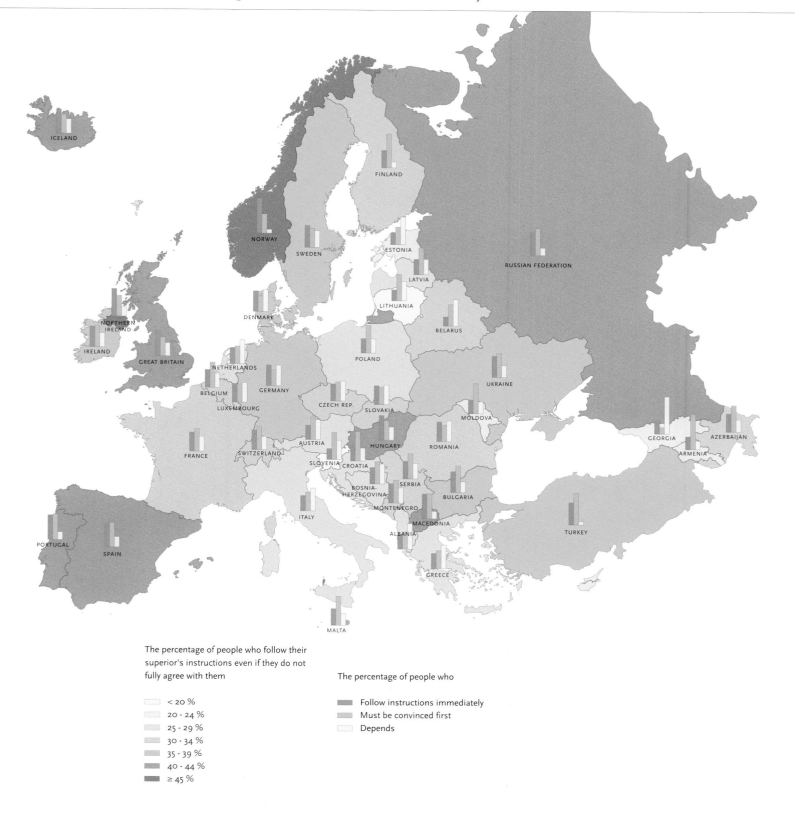

The percentage of people who follow their superior's instructions even if they do not fully agree with them

- ⬜ < 20 %
- 20 - 24 %
- 25 - 29 %
- 30 - 34 %
- 35 - 39 %
- 40 - 44 %
- ≥ 45 %

The percentage of people who

- Follow instructions immediately
- Must be convinced first
- ⬜ Depends

Religion

Many Europeans are proud of it. Some think it is too bad.
However, both agree: Europe is a secularized continent.
Europeans do not go to church anymore, they do not believe
in God anymore, and they do not seem to be religious at all.
Are these assumptions true? It depends. Unmistakable, some
of them are not. One thing is for sure: the old continent is not
as secularized at it seems.

About half of all the Europeans pray or meditate at least once a week. Three out of four Europeans say they are religious persons. Of course, there is a big gap between the more secularized north-western European countries and the more traditional south-eastern ones. However, even in a country like The Netherlands, famous for its liberal tradition, one in four of all the inhabitants attend church. Nevertheless, one assumption is true: most European churches attract fewer believers every year. Especially in the western part of the continent, the old religious institutions are deteriorating. Half a century ago, scholars argued about religion in a 'modernist' way. In pre-modern times, like the Middle Ages, religion was everywhere. One of the effects of modernization,

these scholars thought, is driving back religion finally into the private space of man. Religion is drifting away from politics, from the university, from the arts, from public space in general. Modern man is a rational one, who does not need religion to the extent his ancestors did.

Secularization

Since the German theologian Dietrich Bonhoeffer in 1944 wrote down that secularization meant that 'human beings are growing to maturity', an increasing number of people were positive about this development. The Dutch theologian C.A. van Peursen defined secularization in 1959 as a matter of liberation 'from the religious prison where human reason and language were caught'. It was their assumption

that established religions never would leave their marks on entire civilizations anymore. In their opinions, secularization did not have to defeat or refute religions. Secularization was just ignoring it. Secularization was putting religious worldviews into perspective and made them harmless.

However, Bonhoeffer, Van Peursen and others argued that religion would remain. 'In our secularized era metaphysical problems won't be reduced to silence', theologian Harvey Cox wrote. 'Religion is just going to be a private matter.' A few decades later, their predictions did not come true. All over the world the situation is changing rapidly. Religion is back on stage. In September 2001 fundamentalist Muslims attacked the World Trade Center. In November 2004, the

American president George W. Bush was re-elected because many religious voters backed him. There is no doubt anymore. Religions did not abandon their political agenda. Since the 1990s, we experience 'la revanche de Dieu', as the French scholar Gilles Kepel put it. It is the revenge of God, who returned after a suppressed existence for nearly two centuries of modernization.

Salad bar

There is just one continent that seems to be the exception: Europe. In Europe, Judaism, Christianity, and Islam are still pulled back into the synagogues, churches, and mosques and in the hearts and souls of their followers. In Europe, secularization is still alive, although a growing number of people are worrying about

Largest denomintion

- Roman Catholic/Protestant
- Roman Catholic
- Protestant
- Anglican
- Orthodox
- Muslim

Source: CIA World Factbook 2003

the religious attitude of nearly seventeen million Muslims in the European Union. However, in Europe, religion is still a private matter. Nevertheless, in this private sphere, European religions are very lively.

Whereas confidence in the church is low in the western part of the continent, all over Europe a high percentage of people say they appreciate a religious service on moments of big importance in life. Giving birth, marrying, and dying are still celebrated in a house of worship. Only in the Czech Republic and The Netherlands, will you find less than half of the population which appreciates a religious service. Then again, in Croatia, Ireland, Poland, Romania and the isle of Malta more than 90 percent celebrate their poignant moments in life in church.

Even more interesting is the data about believing, independent from church life. People who consider themselves as atheists are a small minority, except in France, where almost 15 percent say they are atheist. It is obvious that a vast majority of all the Europeans nominate themselves as religious persons. There are even more people who consider themselves as religious as there are people who attend church. It is a kind of 'believing without belonging'. It is significant to know what Europeans believe in. Many believe in non-Christian concepts like reincarnation, lucky charms, and telepathy. It proves religion does not only exist in the doctrines of the classical churches. Europe's religion is like a salad bar. People pick and choose religious beliefs, doctrines and

practices and they are mixing and matching them, as they would select food in a cafeteria. Sociologists talk about this trend as a 'cafeteria religion', or as 'church-free spirituality'. Europeans remain religious, their approach is eclectic, and they borrow ideas from several traditions. Meanwhile many institutionalized churches, especially in the West, are running empty.

Marketing
In short: most of the Europeans who leave church do not loose their religion. This means an increasing number of religious people are outlawed. Perhaps they are willing to be incorporated by new religious institutions. One can wonder whether Europe will keep aloof from the current

worldwide de-secularization. In this respect, it could be interesting to compare Europe with the United States. In the 1970s, both continents seemed to develop in the same way. Secularization took place in Dordogne and the Rocky Mountains. At some point, the tracks went apart.

The most modern of all nation states remained very religious. One of the explanations is the 'market style' approach of many American churches. They compete with each other and look for new opportunities to sell religion. Therefore, they are eager to know and fulfil the religious needs of the American people. One can wonder whether European churches will follow suit one day. However, there is no indication that European secularization is on its return.

Attendance of religious services

Religious services

Percentage of people who appreciate a religious service at death, marriage or birth

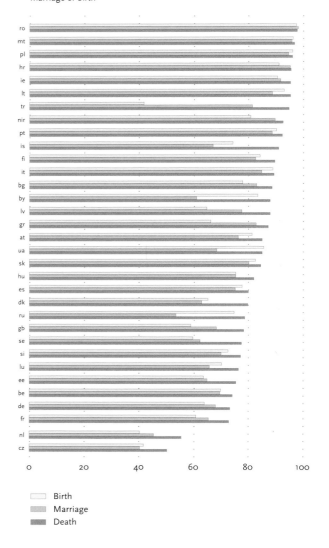

- Birth
- Marriage
- Death

Attendance of religious services according to age

Percentage of people who visit a religious service once a week or more

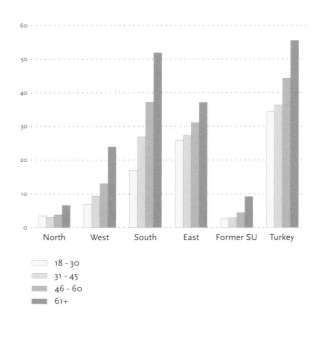

- 18 - 30
- 31 - 45
- 46 - 60
- 61+

Meditation

A small majority of Europeans takes some moments to pray, mediate or contemplate

- No
- Yes

Praying

Percentage of people who pray at least once a week

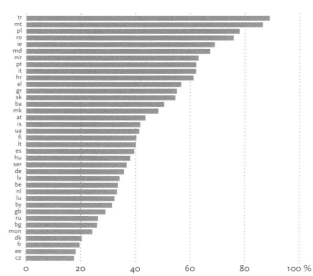

Nearly 40% of Europeans only attend church on special occasions;
30% attend religious services regularly, another 30% never;
yet a large majority of 75% find a religious service appropriate at birth, marriage and death

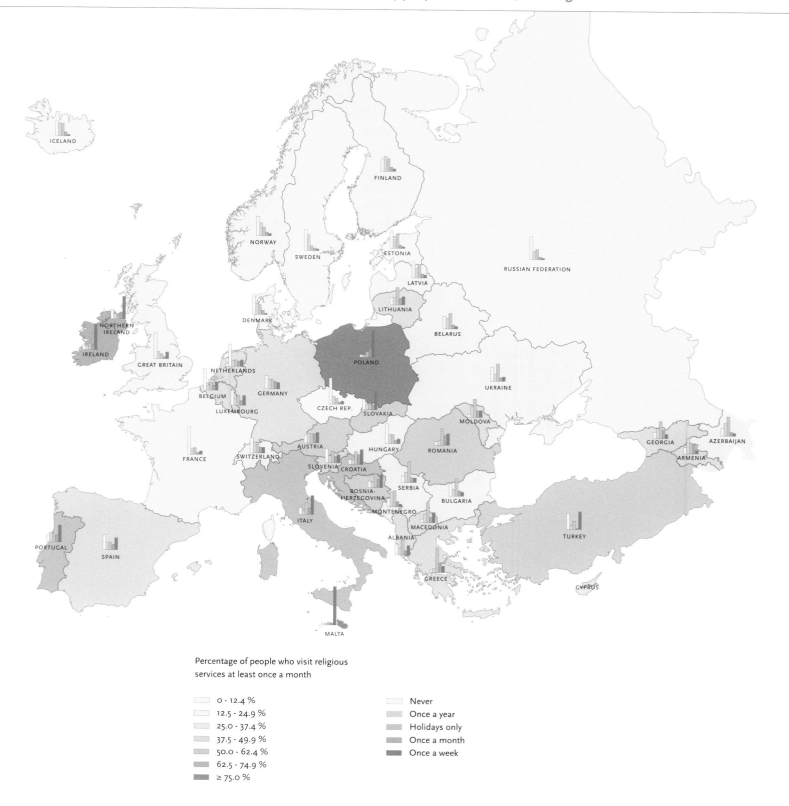

Percentage of people who visit religious
services at least once a month

0 - 12.4 %		Never
12.5 - 24.9 %		Once a year
25.0 - 37.4 %		Holidays only
37.5 - 49.9 %		Once a month
50.0 - 62.4 %		Once a week
62.5 - 74.9 %		
≥ 75.0 %		

Trust in the church

< 2.0
2.0 - 2.3
2.4 - 2.7
2.8 - 3.1
≥ 3.2

Scale 1 (None at all) - 4 (A great deal)

Confidence in the church in Romania and Bulgaria

From a religious perspective, there is a large gap between Romania and Bulgaria. Romanians have a lot of confidence in their church, Bulgarians do not. The Bulgarian province of Severen Tsentralen and the neighbouring Romanian province Sud could not differ more. Severen Tsentralen is as secularised as Estonia or Czech Republic; the people of Sud are committed to the church like in Poland or Malta. In both countries, most of the religious people are Orthodox. In Bulgaria 83 percent is Bulgarian Orthodox; in Romania, 87 percent is Eastern Orthodox. All through the communist decades, both churches suffered from severe suppression. In Bulgaria, state took over control of the church. Figureheads in the Bulgarian church were communist appointed. The Romanian Orthodox Church was subservient too and a tool of the communist government. However, there were some differences. The Hungarian theologist Miklos Tomka describes the way Romanians still emphasized Orthodoxy as 'their' religion.

In Romania, like in Poland and Slovakia, communism did not succeed in liquidating the traditional economy and the rural social system. Where the social system persisted, it maintained traditional culture too. In these countries, communism functioned as an oppressive political superstructure without being able to change the goals, the values and the everyday behaviour of the people. In Bulgaria on the other hand, the Orthodox churches accommodated with the communist regime.

As the American sociologist Mary Gautier argues, these churches were really identified in the eyes of the people as operating in cooperation with the Soviet State. Therefore these churches lost their credibility among religious believers, who then disaffiliated in substantial numbers.

Confidence in the church by denomination

None at all
Not very much
Quite a lot
A great deal

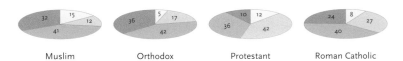

Muslim

Orthodox

Protestant

Roman Catholic

Measuring confidence in the church as an institution is problematic in the Islamic world. There is the word 'church' (the mosque) refers to the 'house of God', that is the building where one prays and attends religious services. The Arabic root of the word mosque can be translated as a "community meeting place". Unlike the Orthodox, Protestant and Roman Catholic faiths, Muslims do not have a central church hierarchy, although within a country often a formal organization exists. An example is the church organization of the Shiites in Iran, with Ayatollah Ali Khamenei as its supreme leader. Most of the Muslims in Europe live in Turkey. Secular Turkey, however, does

not allow independent religious orders or associations which have explicit Islamic aims or objectives. Thus, the Sunni Muslims in Turkey don't have a 'church'. The confidence of Muslims in the church as measured here refers to the trust in Department of Religious Affairs, a Turkish government institution that is responsible for running the mosques, appointing and promoting the mosque personnel and taking care of all the official religions functions.

Churches are not giving adequate answers to today's social problems according to a large majority of Europeans; however they do answer to the spiritual needs

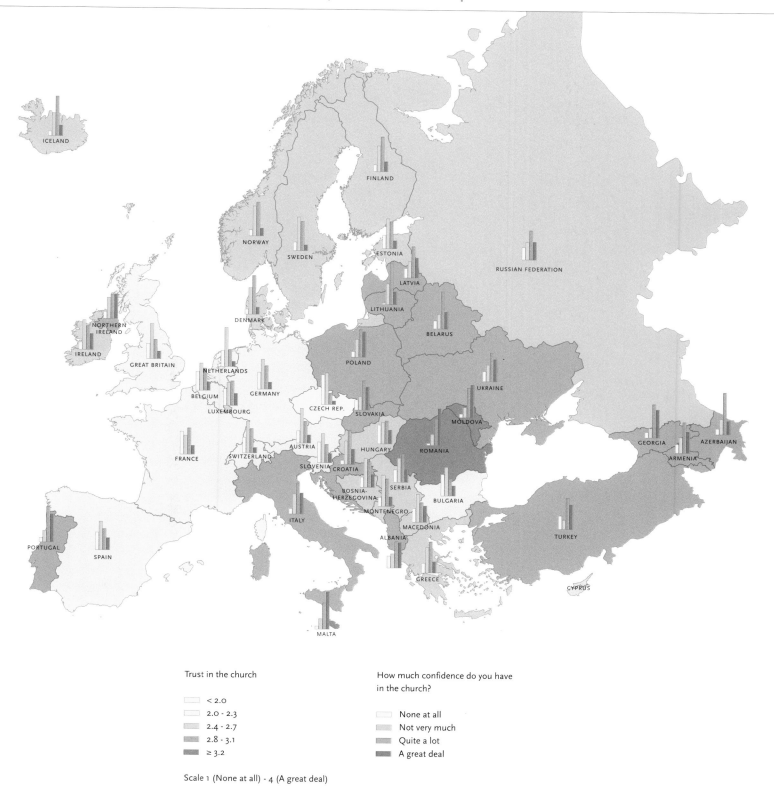

Trust in the church

- ☐ < 2.0
- ☐ 2.0 - 2.3
- ☐ 2.4 - 2.7
- ☐ 2.8 - 3.1
- ☐ ≥ 3.2

Scale 1 (None at all) - 4 (A great deal)

How much confidence do you have
in the church?

- ☐ None at all
- ☐ Not very much
- ☐ Quite a lot
- ☐ A great deal

Importance of God

Believing

Percentage of people who say they are (not) a religious person (independently whether or not they go to church)

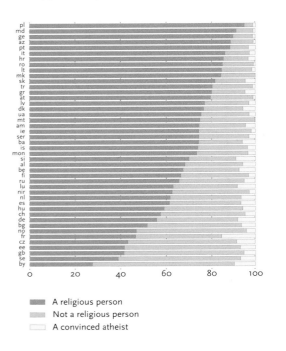

- A religious person
- Not a religious person
- A convinced atheist

The supreme being

Traditional Christian religion explained the origin of the cosmos and human existence in Genesis: God created all life, creatures and the universe in six days. Good and evil, suffering and death were all put in the light of an almighty, supernatural power.

In modern Western society, this traditional religious meaning system is no longer dominant. People are less inclined to approach the origin and meaning of cosmos and human life from a theistic viewpoint. Miracles have become a rarity, and almost every secondary school teaches the Theory of Evolution.

Today's society contains a varied spectrum of meaning systems. In the theistic view, life is governed by God; God is the only source of meaning and interpretation. A more modern view is deism. To deists, daily life is rooted in nature and reason, but they do believe in the existence of a God or Supreme Being;

God is always present but 'in the background'. In the immanentistic view, life is fully governed by the laws of nature and probability, which leaves ample room for a God. Death is inevitable and the meaning of life is that you try to get the best out of it. Still, there is room for some 'life spirit'. Nihilism or atheism is at the other end of the spectrum. Atheist are convinced that there is no God or supernatural life force.

The European Values Study inquired about the images of God (see page 69). Belief in a personal God, that is to say a God that can be addressed by prayer (theistic view), is high in Catholic countries such as Italy, Portugal and Poland. Belief in 'some God, spirit or life force' (deistic view or immanentistic view) is more popular in secular countries such as Czech Republic, the Netherlands and Sweden. Atheism is a minor view throughout Europe.

Believing according to level of education

Percentage of Europeans that say they are (not) religious

- A religious person
- Not a religious person
- A convinced atheist

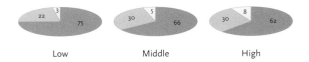

Low — 75, 22, 3
Middle — 66, 30, 5
High — 62, 30, 8

Strength and comfort from religion

Percentage of Europeans who do/don't get strength and comfort from their religion

- No
- Yes

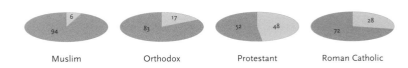

Muslim — 94, 6
Orthodox — 83, 17
Protestant — 52, 48
Roman Catholic — 72, 28

God is most important for the Maltese and Turks; the least for the Czechs

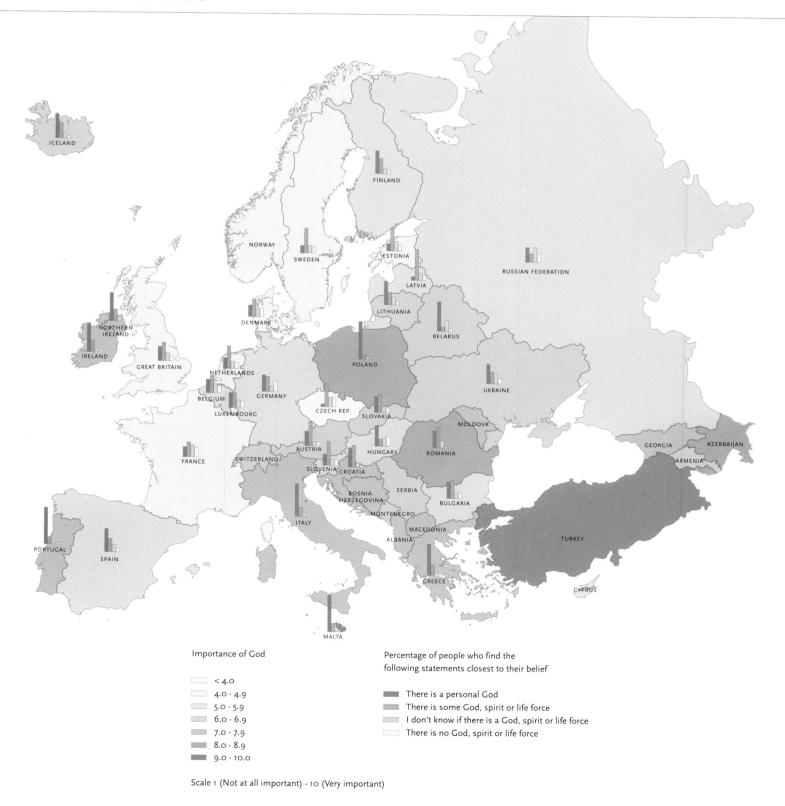

Importance of God

- ☐ < 4.0
- ☐ 4.0 - 4.9
- ☐ 5.0 - 5.9
- ☐ 6.0 - 6.9
- ☐ 7.0 - 7.9
- ☐ 8.0 - 8.9
- ☐ 9.0 - 10.0

Scale 1 (Not at all important) - 10 (Very important)

Percentage of people who find the following statements closest to their belief

- ☐ There is a personal God
- ☐ There is some God, spirit or life force
- ☐ I don't know if there is a God, spirit or life force
- ☐ There is no God, spirit or life force

Traditional beliefs

Hell

Whereas a large majority of Europeans believe in God, the support for the traditional rules and dogmas of the church is diminishing. Especially, the belief in the existence of hell is losing ground, although intra-country differences are high: less than ten percent of the Scandinavians believe in hell, against more than eighty percent of the Maltese, a very religious people. The concept of hell occurs nowhere in the Bible, at least not in the original languages. And for the first thousand years of its existence, hell was not 'taught' in Christian churches. After the Great Schism in 1054 AD, however, Latin theologians surmised that God created a place with purging fires to purify the sinners. Thomas Aquinas (1225-1274), for example, wrote in his Summa Theologica: "That the saints may enjoy their beatitude and the grace of God more abundantly, they are permitted to see the punishment of the damned in hell." Especially in Augustinian theology, hell became an important aspect of Christian belief. It's primary mentor was Augustine of Hippo (354-430) who was strongly influenced by the Greek philosophers. Both Luther and Calvin developed their theologies from Augustine's writings and held the notion of a God that both punishes and rewards.

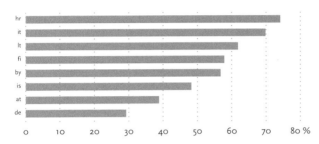

Belief in angels

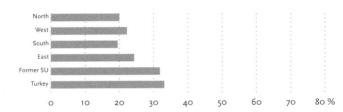

Belief in reincarnation

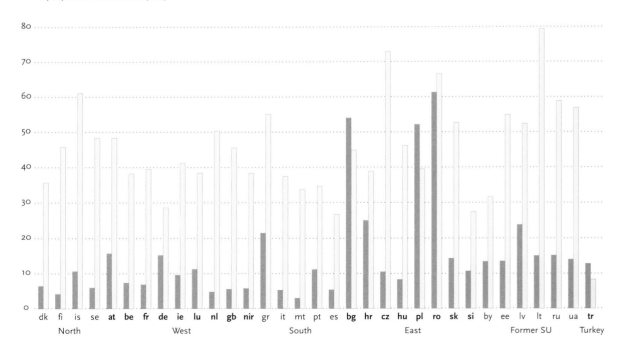

Belief in lucky charm and telepathy

The percentage of people who believe that a lucky charm such as a talisman or mascot protects or helps them and the percentage of people who believe in telepathy

☐ Telepathy
▬ Lucky charm

56.7% of the Azerbaijans believe in angels;
73,7% of the North Irish believe in hell

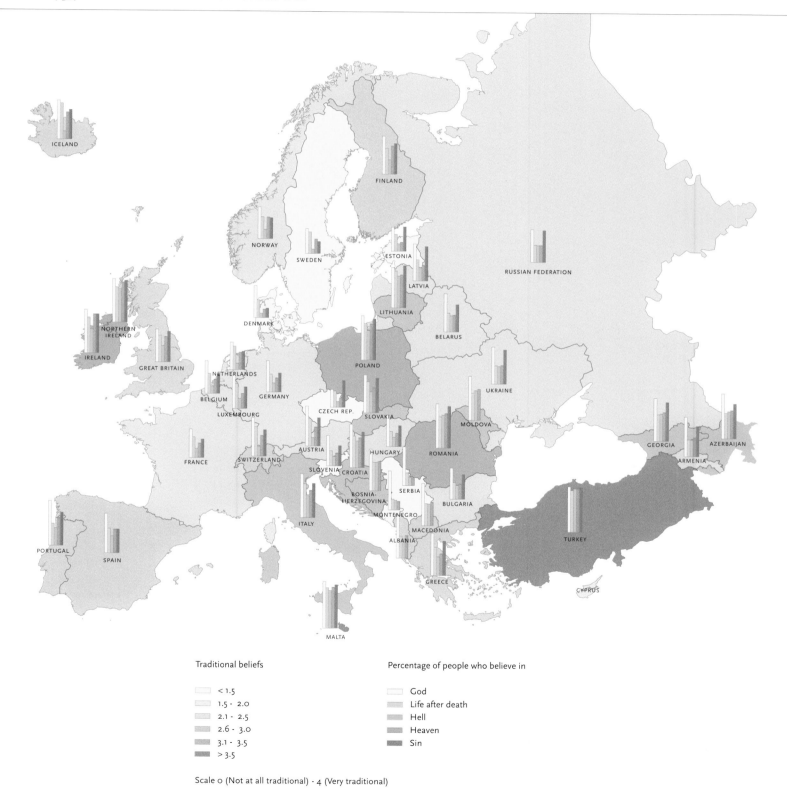

Traditional beliefs

　　　< 1.5
　　　1.5 - 2.0
　　　2.1 - 2.5
　　　2.6 - 3.0
　　　3.1 - 3.5
　　　> 3.5

Scale 0 (Not at all traditional) - 4 (Very traditional)

Percentage of people who believe in

　　　God
　　　Life after death
　　　Hell
　　　Heaven
　　　Sin

Secularization

The percentage of Czechs and Slovaks who state
that they do not belong to any church

☐	0 - 9 %
☐	10 - 19 %
☐	20 - 29 %
☐	30 - 39 %
☐	40 - 49 %
☐	50 - 59 %
☐	≥ 60 %

Secularization in Czech Republic and Slovakia

From 1919 until 1993, Czech Republic and Slovakia have been a
federation. During the Velvet Revolution, they separated. In fact, their
federation had always been a marriage of convenience. During the
twilight of the Habsburg Empire, the Czech in the West and the Slovaks
in the East only united to stand strong against Vienna.
Almost fifty percent of all Czechs are members of a church. Nearly 75
percent of the Slovak are members of a church. From the west to the
east, secularization is gradually slowing down. The Bohemians in the
west are most secularised, the Moravians in the middle are less, and the
residents in the Slovak areas near the Ukraine border are generally church
members who consider themselves as 'religious'. Under the communist
regime, the church was suppressed throughout Czechoslovakia.
The differences in religious attitudes are descending from the late 19th
century. The present day Czech Republic was the most industrialized, best
developed, and most self-conscious part of the Habsburg Empire.
In addition, this part of the Habsburg Empire was governed by Austria.
The increasing Czech rebellion against the Habsburgs went together with
an increasing aversion to the Catholic Church that was closely connected
to 'Vienna'.
On the other hand, present day Slovakia was governed by Hungary, less
developed, poorer and more agricultural. After the Czechs and the Slovaks
merged together to form Czechoslovakia in 1918, a growing number of
Slovaks felt subordinate to the Czechs. The Catholic Church expressed the
sentiments of the Slovaks against the dominant Czech.

--- People's spiritual needs
--- The moral problems
--- The problems of family life
--- The social problems

Church and today's problems
The percentage of people who feel churches
are giving adequate answers to:

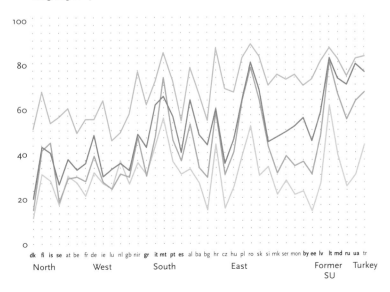

In Moldavia and Poland 93.4% of the people are religious and belong to a church;
only in the Czech Republic and Estonia a (small) majority are not religious

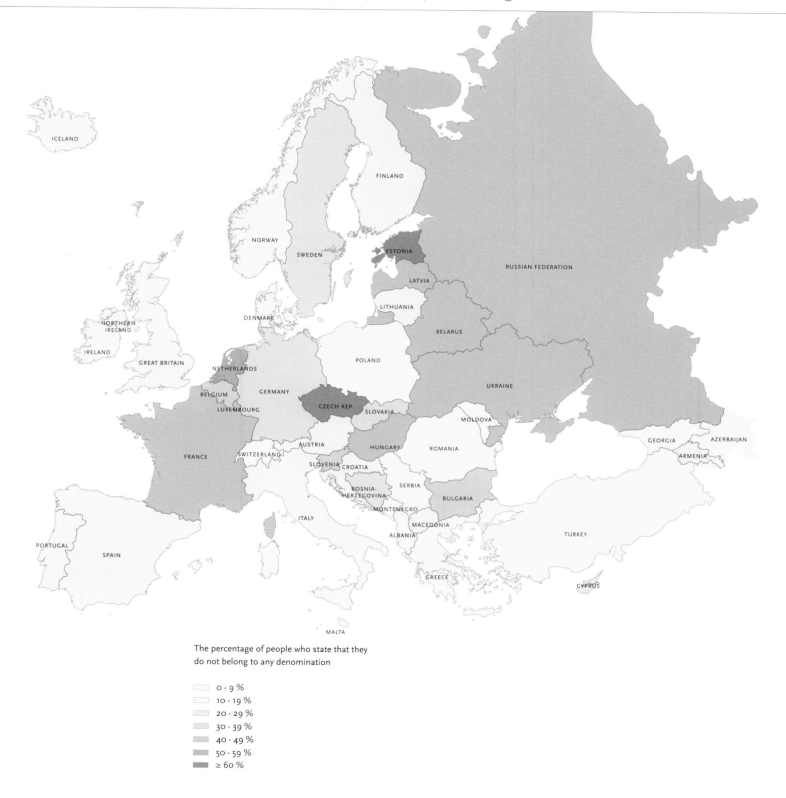

The percentage of people who state that they
do not belong to any denomination

	0 - 9 %
	10 - 19 %
	20 - 29 %
	30 - 39 %
	40 - 49 %
	50 - 59 %
	≥ 60 %

(Not) churchgoing - (not) religious

Percentage of people who are (not) churchgoing and (not) religious

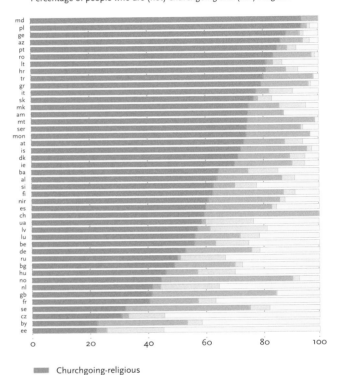

- ▨ Churchgoing-religious
- ▨ Churchgoing-not religious
- ▨ Not churchgoing-religious
- ▨ Not churchgoing-not religious

Europe is not at all as secularised as many people believe. The vast majority of the Europeans are not only member of a church but also consider themselves religious. Vanguards of religious and churched Europeans are Eastern European countries like Moldova, Poland, Georgia, Romania and Azerbaijan. Most secular countries are located in the West. Czech republic is an exception in the sense that it appears most secular. This figure undermines the assumption that Europe is very secularised. Moreover, it reveals an interesting discrepancy in 'church members' and 'believers'. This means there is a certain percentage of Europeans who are not religious, but who consider themselves as member of the church. In reverse, there are many religious people, who are not a member of the church. Especially in countries like Sweden, Norway, Switzerland, or Great Britain the number of people who belong to a church is much larger than the number of people who consider themselves as religious. The British sociologist Grace Davie described this situation as 'belonging without believing.' One of the explanations of

'belonging without believing' is the existence of state churches. In several state churches, everybody is automatically a member of the church and paying a kind of 'church tax'. However, most of the inhabitants consider their church membership as a part of their national identity and not as a religious issue. On the other side: in most of the European countries, particularly in The Netherlands, Estonia, and Czech Republic, there are more people who call themselves religious than there are members of the church. This is called 'believing without belonging'. At least one can conclude religious institutions and religious people are not completely geared to each other. Sociologists further observe not only the decline of institutionalised religiosity that is of churches since the 1960s but also a decline of several secular institutions such as political parties, trade unions and the wide range of leisure activities that require 'gathering' on a regular basis. Reduction in church life in Western Europe should be seen as a part of a profound change in the nature of social life and not as a simple indicator of religious indifference.

Commitment to the church

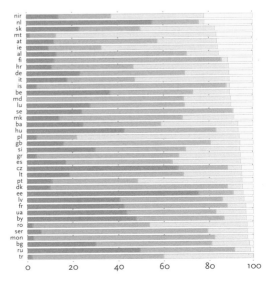

- ▨ No members
- ▨ Marginal members
- ▨ Modal members
- ▨ Core members

Commitment to the church is divided in four typologies:

1. Non-members: no membership to a church or denomination.
2. Marginal members: church members who attend religious services less than once a month.
3. Modal member: church members, who attend religious services at least once a month.
4. Core member: church members, who attend religious services at least once a month and are otherwise involved in church organisations.

The groups of non-members and marginal church-members are largest in the Baltic state of Estonia and the Czech Republic. The opposite is found in Poland and Malta. Here membership, as well as frequent church attendance, is widespread. Intriguing is the unique situation of The Netherlands. More than half of the Dutch population is not a member of a church while on the other hand more than twenty percent is a core church-member.

"European churches are running on empty.
But there is an increasing market for suppliers in new religious thoughts,
institutions, rites and texts."

Theo Schepens
Associate Professor of Sociology of Religion

Dr. Theo M.M. Schepens is an
associate professor Sociology of
Religion at the Faculty of Theology
at Tilburg University.
Contact: theo.schepens@uvt.nl

"It is not so easy to talk about 'secularisation' without a fine-tuned definition. In popular speech secularisation means the number of people that belong to a church or attend church is dropping. Just a short browse through this chapter shows countries like Estonia, the Czech Republic, and the Netherlands as exceptionally secular compared with Poland, Malta or Ireland which are largely religious.

However, figures are not as obvious as they look. In Sweden, for example, 76 percent belongs to a church because, until recently, the Swedish church was a state church. However: in daily life, only about 9 percent of the population actually attends church, and less than 40 percent of the Swedes consider themselves as religious. In the Netherlands, less than half of the Dutch are members of the church, but 26 percent attend church. Even more interesting is the high percentage of people in the Netherlands who indicate they are religious persons, more than 60 percent. In short: the number of the church members, or even the number of people attending a church, gives some indication, but does not fully indicate how religious people are. Sociologists of religion are studying the relationships between religious feelings and connections to a church. The American scholar Rodney Stark developed one of the most attractive views. He is talking about a 'free market in religious ideas' and about 'churches as suppliers of religion'. Free markets in religion arise, as soon as there is freedom of religion. The old churches will have to compete with new suppliers like sects, New Age movements or immigrating religions like Islam. For the traditional churches, this situation is threatening. They maintained a monopoly for centuries, so they did not have to work hard for their success. In fact: many monopolists became a little bit lazy. Challenged by the new, forceful brands, they would like to undercut them, but cannot find the strength to do so.

Now the established churches are running empty. Many Europeans are moved away from the old institutions and established a market for new suppliers. All over Europe, you discover newcomers offering consolation, forgiveness, rites, celebrations, and grand stories about life and death. Jehovah's witnesses, Buddhism, Bahai, Seventh Day Adventist, Soka Gakkai, Mormons, Osho - the former Baghwan movement - et cetera.

Interesting is the rise of Islam in Europe. About 17 million Muslims are living inside the European Union and their number is growing. Their birth rate is far beyond the moderate birth rate in the Union and many Muslims still move into Europe. Moreover, there is an opportunity for Islam to grow by converting non-Muslims. Imagine a young person with religious needs. A boy who is raised in a lukewarm Christian family, who is visiting half-empty churches and who doubts about all the old certainties. One day this youngster meets young Muslims. They consider their faith as hot, their houses of worship are full; they do not have any doubts about their religious beliefs. Well, our young boy has never experienced this kind of religion and will be fascinated by it. What keeps him from joining the new community? The more powerful and stuffed a religious movement is, the higher the price you have to pay to join it, the more attractive it is. On a 'free market in religious ideas' the strong ones will survive, the weak and insubstantional ones will be defeated.

Religious animals

Not everybody is in favour of this approach. People think it is not possible to argue about a 'religious economy'. Religion is something you cannot conceive as a commodity. Sure, you cannot compare God's Mercy with a pair of shoes. The model of a 'religious economy' is only an attempt to understand the changes of religious preference from a supply-side perspective. It addresses institutionalised religions or religious ideas at a level of production. It assumes religions are firms, like the churches, the sects or the 'New Age movements' that are producing symbols, texts, phrases and rites. These religious firms compete with each other to attract followers.

Nevertheless, this is only one side. The model of religious economy contains another assumption: there is a relatively stable demand side. People are continuously looking for religious institutions or religious ideas. However, it is hardly an assumption anymore. History has shown human beings as religious animals. For ages people ask themselves questions about the meaning of life, the meaning of death or the meaning of suffering and injustice. The only ones who are able to answer these questions definitively are the gods. Hitherto, it is an assumption that there will eventually be a future without religion."

Politics

'Oh, east is east and west is west / and never the twain shall meet' is the famous opening of Rudyard Kiplings Ballad of East and West. A quick look at the maps and statistics on the political situation in West and East Europe seem to underline this observation.

Western democracies are much older than Eastern ones. The East is less willing to join in political actions than the West. Support for democracy is high in the West and low in the Eastern parts of Europe. West is a 'post-materialistic' society, East is 'materialistic'. In a nutshell: it seems the Iron Curtain did not disappear, the curtain is only raised a little bit. Nevertheless, a closer look unlocks a more complex phenomenon.

Battle lines

In 1989, the American political scientist Francis Fukuyama wrote his well read 'The End of History and the Last Man'. Arguing from a philosophical point of view, he stated the whole world was ready to jump into liberalism and democracy. Since the wars in the former Yugoslavia, Congo, Afghanistan and Iraq,

Fukuyama's ideas fell into discredit. Fukuyama's successor was another American political scientist, Samuel Huntington. In 1993, he published the article 'The clash of civilizations' and denied Fukuyama's development towards liberalism and democracy. Huntington saw a lot of conflict in the post 1989 world. The dominating source of these conflicts would be cultural. 'The fault lines between civilizations will be the battle lines of the future', he predicted. Moreover, one of these fault lines is the boundary between Christianity in the West and in the East Islam and Orthodox Christianity. A boundary will split Europe in two parts, cutting right through Belarus, Ukraine and former Yugoslavia. Since the attack on the World Trade Center in 2001, sceptics honour Huntington as a modern prophet, and definitely

put Fukuyama aside as a fool. However, it was Fukuyama's prophecy that came true on the European continent. Half of all the European countries have changed into democracies since the Berlin Wall came down. Fukuyama's theory is vulnerable on the philosophical level, because nobody can be sure the new democracies will not change into totalitarian states again. Yet, in the aftermath of the revolutions in 1989, Fukuyama showed the world how people in former communist states are longing for freedom, participation, and democracy. When researchers all over Europe ask people about the statement 'Democracy may have its problems but is better than any other form of government', the common consent is overwhelming. More than 90 percent of the Europeans subscribe to this point of view. In general, Europe still deserves

the designation 'the cradle of democracy.'

Blurring differences

Nevertheless, there are big differences. Support for democracy is strong in Western Europe, especially in Norway, Iceland and Denmark. Heading East, support for democracy is slowing down. In the Russian Federation and the former Soviet States of Estonia and Latvia, only one person in five thinks a democratic system is 'very good'. Still, two out of three Russians are backing up their recently achieved democracy. Do we have to worry? No, we do not. People's distance to democracy in Eastern European countries can be explained. Firstly, some democracies in the East are, according to Western standards, very poor. In the Russian Federation freedom of press is limited, political opponents

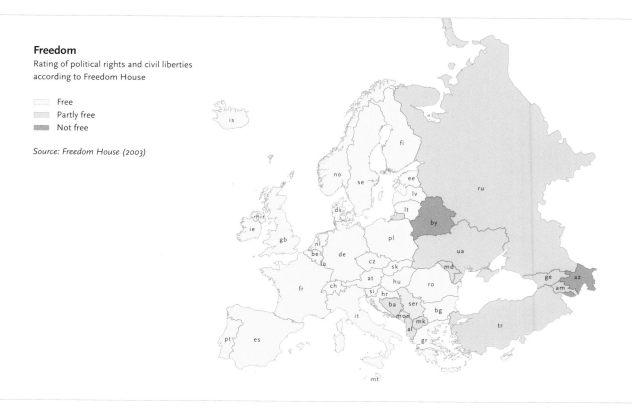

Freedom

Rating of political rights and civil liberties
according to Freedom House

- ☐ Free
- ☐ Partly free
- ▉ Not free

Source: Freedom House (2003)

are thwarted and democratic institutions like the Russian parliament are weak. Secondly, in Eastern Europe democracy is still very young. The tsars did not allow any democratic involvement; neither did the communist's 'red tsars'. Establishing confidence in a democratic state is a process which takes several years. Thirdly, during the communist regime, democracy represented hope. Not knowing what democracy actually can achieve, people thought a democratic society would solve their problems. They didn't take into account a long period of transition, including fear, agitation and social unrest. They could not foresee unemployment and widening gaps between the rich and the poor. More than a decade after the end of communism, they exchanged hope for realism. Considering this, it is encouraging that more than sixty percent of

all Russians subscribe to the idea that 'Democracy may have its problems, but is better than any other form of government'.

Optimistic
Instead of analysing the relative lack of support for democracy in Eastern Europe, you can ask another question - Why are so many people in the West supporting democracy? A plausible explanation is: westerners are used to democracy. The majority were born after World War II and they did not experience any other form of government. In addition, everybody who remembers fascism and national socialism has even better reasons to vote for democracy.
In spite of this, not everybody in the West is very eager to maintain the democratic achievements. Especially in the southern part of Europe, there is a lack of interest

in politics. This is even worse in Great Britain and Ireland. Less than thirty percent of the Anglo-Saxons follow politics every day through television, radio or newspapers.
However, asking people in Europe about the importance of politics in their life, the assumed differences between West and East are fading away. It is only possible to single out separate countries, and ask why people in nations like Armenia or the Netherlands think politics are very important. Alternatively, how to explain the comparable outcome in both France and the Russian Federation, although these countries do not have lot in common?
In spite of all the differences, a closer look at all the characteristics between West and East reveals a continent where the real differences, caused by the Iron

Curtain, are blurring. Everybody knows the famous start of Kipling's Ballad of East and West. Only a few remember the optimistic end. But there is neither East nor West, Border, nor Breed, nor Birth / When two strong men stand face to face, tho' they come from the ends of the earth!

Importance of politics

European Parliament

The European Union is more than a confederation, but less than a federation. There is a Council of Ministers, in which the governments of the member states are represented. There is the European Parliament, directly elected by the citizens of every country. And there is the European Commission, the daily government, which must take into account the Parliament's majority. There are, however, often complaints about the large distance between European citizens and the institutions. This distance has a special term: the European 'democratic deficit'. Although many political scientists are convinced that the main 'democratic deficit' in the European Union is psychological, not institutional, evidence for the democratic deficit is found in the dropping turnout of the European elections.

The first elections for the European Parliament took place in 1979 and drew 63% of the voters. In 1999, the turnout fell below 50% and the latest elections (June 2004) only attracted 45.7% of the voters (160 million votes). The turnout in the fifteen older EU-countries was about the same in the 2004 election as in the previous one. However, in the ten new member states the average was a mere 27%. Within the fifteen older member states, turnout trends vary widely. Participation is highest where voting is compulsory (Belgium 91%, Greece 63% and Luxembourg 89%) but is also traditionally high in Italy (73%). Malta and Cyprus bucked the trend among new member states in 2004, with turnouts of 82% and 71% respectively. Turnouts were lowest in Slovakia (17%) and Poland (21%).

Political interest

How interested are you in politics?

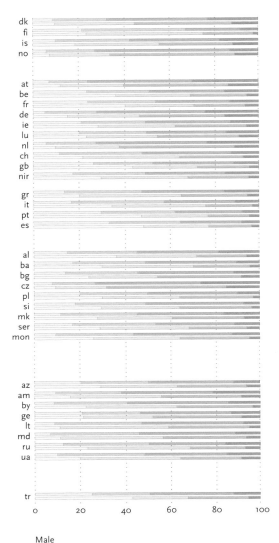

Male
- ▫ Not at all interested
- ▪ Not very interested
- ▪ Somewhat interested
- ▪ Very interested

Female
- ▫ Not at all interested
- ▫ Not very interested
- ▪ Somewhat interested
- ▪ Very interested

Discussing politics

When you get together with your friends, how often do you discuss political matters?

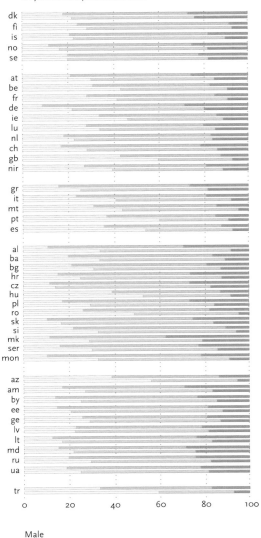

Male
- ▫ Never
- ▪ Occasionally
- ▪ Frequently

Female
- ▫ Never
- ▫ Occasionally
- ▪ Frequently

Wealth and political interest

A minimal degree of political interest among citizens is an important precondition for the stability and development of democratic political societies. Usually, political interest is depicted as personal 'trait' that can be explained by variances in peoples resources and skills. Nevertheless, the social scientists Jan van Deth and Martin Elff used Eurobarometer data to search for factors explaining inter country differences in political interest or apathy, relying on the assumption that government intervention can activate political interest and that contextual factors need to be taken into account. Their principal conclusion is that politicisation (for example openness of the political system or control capacity of the state) does not play an important role in the explanation of cross-national differences in political interest in Europe. Socio-economic development, however, does: the higher the level of socio-economic development, the higher the aggregate level of political involvement and the lower the level of political apathy.

Source: www.mzes.uni-mannheim.de

Importance of politics

Percentage of people who indicate politics as "very or quite important" in their life

- < 20 %
- 20 - 29 %
- 30 - 39 %
- 40 - 49 %
- ≥ 50 %

Political interest according to age

Percentage of people who are (very) interested in politics

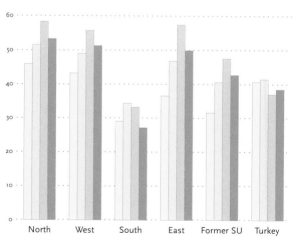

- 18 - 30
- 31 - 45
- 46 - 60
- 61+

Politics in daily life

Percentage of people who follow politics every day through television, radio or newspapers

- < 30 %
- 30 - 39 %
- 40 - 49 %
- 50 - 59 %
- 60 - 69 %
- ≥ 70 %

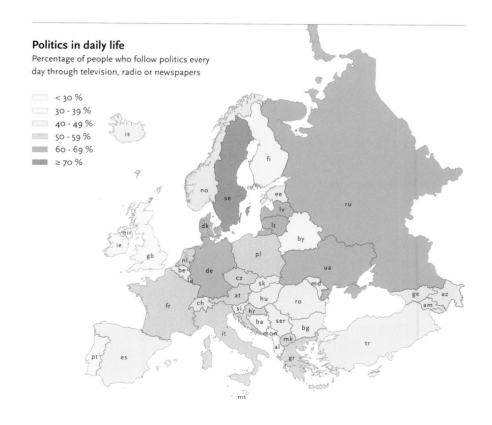

Willingness to join in political actions

Willingness to join in various political actions

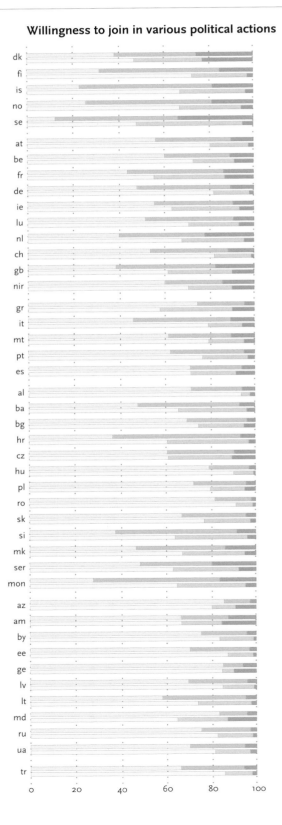

Joining in boycotts
- Would never do
- Might do
- Have done

Joining in unofficial strikes
- Would never do
- Might do
- Have done

dk, fi, is, no, se, at, be, fr, de, ie, lu, nl, ch, gb, nir, gr, it, mt, pt, es, al, ba, bg, hr, cz, hu, pl, ro, sk, si, mk, ser, mon, az, am, by, ee, ge, lv, lt, md, ru, ua, tr

0   20   40   60   80   100

Membership of political parties/groups
Percentage of people who belong to a political party or group

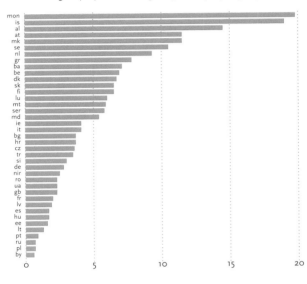

mon, is, al, at, mk, se, nl, gr, ba, be, dk, sk, fi, lu, mt, ser, md, ie, it, bg, hr, cz, tr, si, de, nir, ro, ua, gb, fr, lv, es, hu, ee, lt, pt, ru, pl, by

0   5   10   15   20

Willingness in Europe to sign petitions

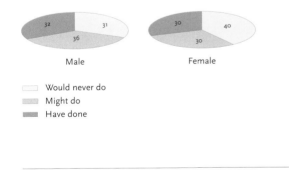

Male: 32, 36, 31
Female: 30, 30, 40

- Would never do
- Might do
- Have done

Willingness in Europe to occupy buildings or factories

Male: 15, 82, 3
Female: 9, 89, 2

- Would never do
- Might do
- Have done

27% of Greeks have occupied buidings or factories, a political action that 97% of the Albanians would never join in

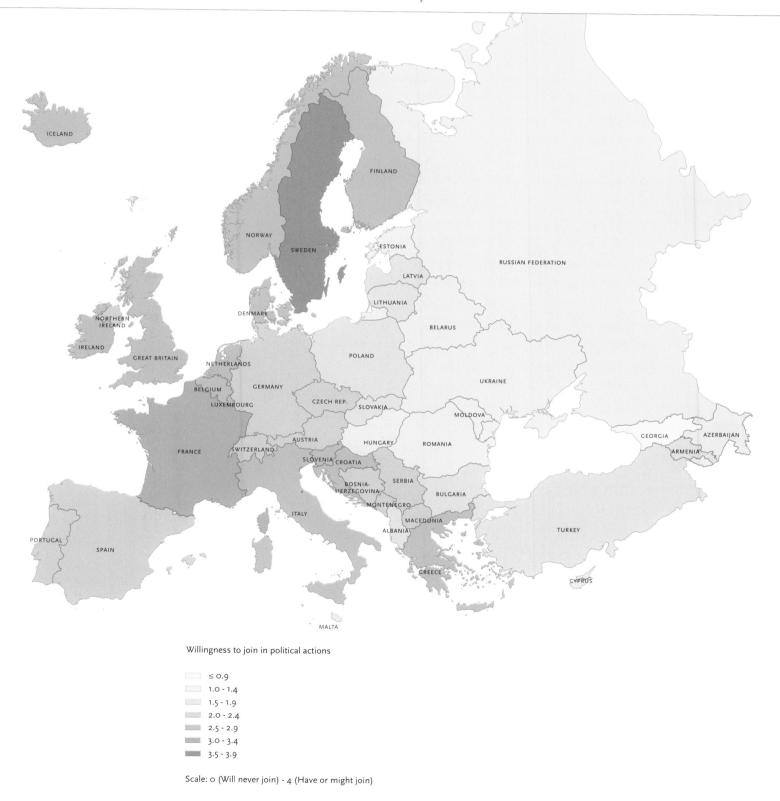

Willingness to join in political actions

- ≤ 0.9
- 1.0 - 1.4
- 1.5 - 1.9
- 2.0 - 2.4
- 2.5 - 2.9
- 3.0 - 3.4
- 3.5 - 3.9

Scale: 0 (Will never join) - 4 (Have or might join)

Political views

Left and right

A well-known and frequently used concept to identify and classify political views in Europe is the distinction of left and right. Left and right are regarded as the extreme poles of an ideological dimension indicative of someone's political and societal ideas and opinions. Left is generally identified as progressive, in favour of social change and equality, whereas right is seen in favour of retaining status quo, conservative and against more equality in society. But the idea of left and right varies from country to country, and part of the concept lies in the eye of the beholder: a 'leftist' person tends to view a left party less left than someone who is right. The polarization between left and right not only applies to political conflicts; the different outlooks also appear in all kinds of social moral and ethical issues such as abortion, euthanasia, nuclear energy,

asylum seeking etcetera. Left is regarded to take the sides of the poor, the disadvantaged, the deprived and minority groups; they are most concerned about the environment and opposed to nuclear energy and arms, and in moral issues left represents the liberal stances. Right is commonly seen as nationalistic, and is associated with the conservative and traditional standpoints. They are the strongest proponents of authority, order, and a restrictive moral. Although the left-right polarity is persuasively used in Europe and recognized as a useful conceptual tool to categorize political views, research shows that left and right are not robust indicators of ideological orientations towards all social, moral and political issues within societies. Political views cannot be captured in a single dimension. And as such, this classification should be used carefully.

Political involvement according to political colour

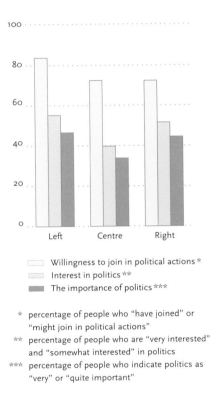

Willingness to join in political actions *
Interest in politics **
The importance of politics ***

* percentage of people who "have joined" or "might join in political actions"
** percentage of people who are "very interested" and "somewhat interested" in politics
*** percentage of people who indicate politics as "very" or "quite important"

Personal freedom versus equality

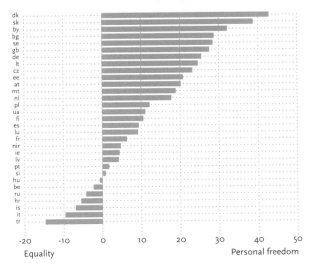

Equality — Personal freedom

Two statements were put forward: A: "I find that both freedom and equality are important. But if I were to choose one or the other, I would consider personal freedom more important, that is, everyone can live in freedom and develop without hindrance" and B: "Certainly both freedom and equality are important. But if I were to choose one or the other, I would consider equality more important, that is, that nobody is underprivileged and that social class differences are not so strong."
Here is presented the percentage of people who prefer statement A minus the percentage who prefer B. In this way countries are ordered according to their appreciation of personal freedom versus equality.

Of all European people, the Danish most strongly emphasize personal development;
for the Turkish the fact that nobody is underprivileged is more important

Political views

Political views on a left-right scale

- ≤ 4.5
- 4.6 - 5.0
- 5.1 - 5.5
- 5.6 - 6.0
- ≥ 6.1

Scale 1 (Left)- 10 (Right)

Levelling off incomes

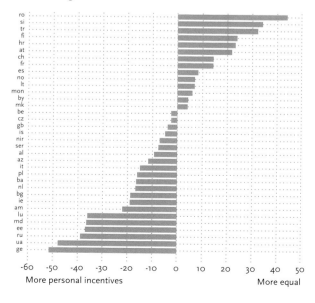

People were asked to place their views
on a scale of 1 to 10 in which 1 stands for
"incomes should be made more equal"
and 10 stands for "there should be greater
incentives for individual effort".
Here is given the percentage of people who
choose "1, 2 or 3" minus the percentage who
choose "8, 9 or 10". In this way countries are
ordered according to their appreciation for
levelling off incomes.

Personal initiative versus state care

The welfare state

In modern welfare states, individuals and families are guaranteed a minimum income. There is a national safety net that protects people against poverty due to sickness, unemployment and old age. Furthermore, the welfare state provides a certain degree of social services: health care, scholarships, housing benefit etc. Wanted or unwanted, the welfare state hereby modifies the play of market forces.

The welfare state may be called a European 'invention'. It roots in the late 19th century, when Britain launched its factory legislation and Germany initiated a national compulsory insurance against sickness, accidents, old age and invalidity. It is predominantly based on a radical transformation in the attitude towards poverty. The poor were no longer considered poor because of their own fault, but because of tendencies within the market system and thus society has an obligation to take care of them. Before, people in need depended on family, friends, the church or charity.

Before the Second World War, economic conditions in Europe were hard, preventing the welfare state from developing quickly. Soon after the Second World War, however, democracy and the social power of the growing working class grew. This was seen especially in the 1960s and 1970s, when the welfare state matured thanks to growing economic prosperity.

The range of social services provided for by the welfare state depends on the balance between national economical and social forces. Within Europe, social expenditure is highest in Scandinavian countries (around 30% of GDP in Sweden, Denmark, and Finland) and lowest in Eastern countries (around 10% in Turkey, Russia and Bulgaria).

Today, there is ample debate about the (retreating) welfare state. One reason is that, due to the ageing European population, health care services and state-provided pensions put large pressure on the national budgets. But there are also more principal objections to the welfare state. Social security would discourage people to search for a job, even make them lazy, and the welfare state would hollow out important social structures and family networks, thereby eroding informal solidarity and civic morality. The latter effect has been studied by social scientists from Tilburg University on the basis of European Values Study's data. They found a high positive correlation between a country's level of welfare spending and levels of social capital. However, this is no final proof of a beneficial effect of the welfare state on society, because it is not clear what came first: the welfare state or social capital? In addition, high social expenditure was found to have a negative impact on people's informal solidarity. This, however, is also not evidence for a moral "evil" effect of the welfare state. The citizens of welfare states appear not to worry about needy people, because they believe that the state will take care of them, not because they wouldn't care for each other. Thus, the relation between welfare state and civic morality remains complex.

Greater emphasis on the development of the individual is ...

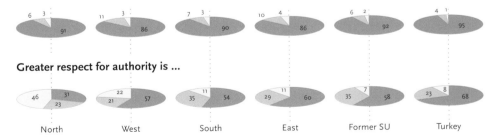

- A good thing
- I don't mind
- A bad thing

Greater respect for authority is ...

North West South East Former SU Turkey

In contrast to the rest of Europe, the Northern part finds that a greater respect for authority would be a bad development

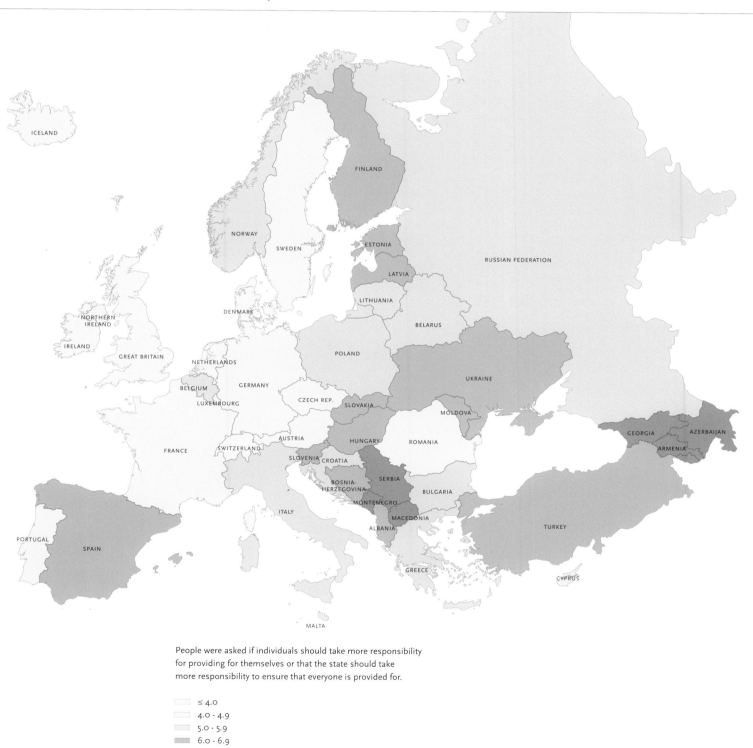

People were asked if individuals should take more responsibility for providing for themselves or that the state should take more responsibility to ensure that everyone is provided for.

≤ 4.0
4.0 - 4.9
5.0 - 5.9
6.0 - 6.9
≥ 7.0

Scale 1 (More individual responsibility) - 10 (More state responsibility)

Individual responsibility

People were asked to place their views on three statements on
a scale of 1 to 10 in which 1 stands for a statement in favour of more
personal initiative and 10 for more state care and control.
Here is given the percentage of people who chose 1, 2 or 3 minus the
percentage who chose 8, 9 or 10. In this manner a measure is
found for the degree in which a country prefers individual
responsibility above state control.

Statement: "The state should give more freedom
to firms" versus "The state should control firms
more effectively"

Statement: "Competition is good; it stimulates
people to work hard and develop new ideas"
versus "Competition is harmful; it brings out
the worst in people"

Statement: "People who are unemployed
should have to take any job available or
loose their unemployment benefits" versus
"People who are unemployed should have
the right to refuse a job they do not want"

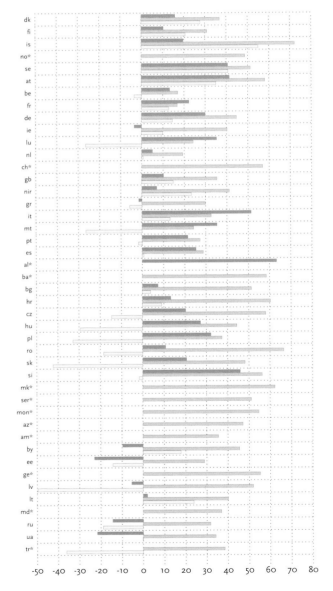

* incomplete data

"European nation states are democracies, but the European Union is not a democracy"

Willem Witteveen
Professor of Jurisprudence

Prof. Dr. Willem J. Witteveen is a professor of Jurisprudence at the Faculty of Law at Tilburg University and member of the Senate of The Netherlands.
Contact: w.j.witteveen@uvt.nl

"Are European countries democracies? The formal answer is yes. Of course, the 25 member states within the European Union are democracies. Nevertheless, nowadays even Russia, Georgia or Moldova are changing their leaders through elections. It is even more encouraging to see how many people all over Europe agree with the idea there is no better form of government than democracy. The percentage is more than 90 percent in most of the countries, with over 60 percent agreeing in Russia.

However, there are several aspects to worry about. One of them is the low percentage of people who belong to a political party, movement or group. It is not only a very small percentage in former communist states such as Russia, Poland or Belarus. Even in core states of the European Union, like the United Kingdom, France or Germany, less than four percent of the citizens belong to a political movement. We have to ask ourselves what democracy means. Because democracy is not limited to free elections every four or five years.

First, democracy means 'representation'. A long time ago, in class-ridden societies, citizens elected the ones who represented them and left governing to their leaders until the next election. Today people like to be heard, they ask their leaders to listen and represent them continuously. Representation requires politicians who are good listeners. However, it does not assume active citizens. Therefore, strong democracies need 'participation'. They require an active approach by their citizens. Participating citizens like to chat on the Internet about politics. They analyse problems and they come up with new solutions. They write letters to the editor of their newspapers and they demonstrate on the streets when they do not agree.

Transparency

Representation, participation... we are not through yet. Another aspect of democracy is 'deliberation', weighing the pros and cons at several places in society. Many problems are very complex and cannot be solved by a small group of decision makers alone. In addition, democracy demands a 'balance of power'. People, who are invested with authority, need to be controlled. By the judiciary of course, and by organising referendums or by involving independent citizens. The long and the short of a full democracy is a specific kind of mentality. It is the willingness to share power, to include everybody in the political process.

According to these criteria, most of the countries in the European Union have to be ranked as very democratic. Nevertheless, there are differences. Compare, for instance, the most southern and most northern countries in the Union: Italy and Sweden.

The latter is very transparent; in Sweden, there are many discussions about legislation. People in the government are in close contact with their voters. The result is a population that sticks to the law because the Swedes are convinced everybody benefits from it.

Italy, on the other hand, is not transparent at all. Although elected, a small elite in the government is ruling the country. Throughout Italy, there is always an attempt to dodge the regulations, because not everybody is convinced about the necessity of the rules. Nevertheless, in Italy democracy works too. Next to the official democracy on paper, you can find a grey circuit where people are discussing, considering what to do, negotiating and organising their lives.

Democracies are vulnerable. Even old democracies are. A threat to European democracies is the uncontrolled power of the European Union. Everybody knows a majority of national laws are produced in Brussels.

However, most of the national parliaments do not show real interest in European politics. It is too complex and national affairs swallow up lots of political energy. Many Members of Parliament in European capitals are faced with more or less fixed solutions in the European council. Their ministers will return from Brussels with new legislation, admitting the quality is not excellent. Nevertheless, they will persuade the Members of Parliament that this is the best compromise they could get. They leave the Members of Parliament just one choice: to cooperate. But the MPs are right to argue that the Council has excluded them.

Looking at representation, participation, deliberation and balancing powers, the European Union is no democracy at all. National parliaments miss the skills and information to counterbalance the European Council. Although the European Parliament is gaining power, it remains still too powerless."

Post-materialism

| 1.0 - 1.2 |
| 1.3 - 1.5 |
| 1.6 - 1.8 |
| 1.9 - 2.2 |
| 2.2 - 2.4 |
| 2.5 - 2.7 |
| 2.8 - 3.0 |

Scale 1 (Materialistic society) - 3 (Post-materialistic society)

Post-materialism in Spain and Portugal

The post-materialism theory in social science states that growing levels of economic prosperity gradually induces a shift from materialism to post-materialism in advanced industrial societies. Economic and physical security allows people to give priority to 'higher' needs and values related to quality of life issues, self-realisation, environmentalism and social concerns such as minority rights, fair trade, gender equality and the like. And indeed, the European Values Studies find a solid correlation between national Gross Domestic Product and levels of post-materialism (see page 89). However, wealth does not explain all variations in levels of post-materialism. On the country level, Spain and Portugal 'score' as may be expected on the basis of their national incomes: Spain is close to the more rich North-Western part of Europe; Portugal resembles the 'poorer' Eastern countries. On a regional level, however, the link between GDP and post-materialism is weaker. Within Portugal, the Algarve is the least post-materialistic region. Yet, except for Lisboa e Vale do Tejo, this is the most wealthy region in Portugal. In Spain, Cantabria may not be among the wealthiest regions, but it is far more prosperous than Extremadura or Andalucia.

Less emphasis on money and material possessions is ....

- A good thing
- I don't mind
- A bad thing

North   West   South   East   Former SU   Turkey

Post-materialism according to age
Scale 1 (Materialistic society) - 3 (Post-materialistic society)

- 18 - 30
- 31 - 45
- 46 - 60
- 61+

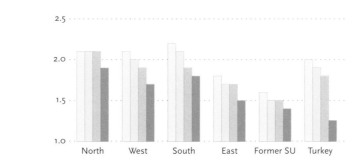

Large changes in a society's value pattern often result from younger generations having a more modern value set than the previous generations, rather than from people changing their opinions and beliefs. Post-materialism appears no exception to this rule, as can be seen from this graph. Clearly, European regions are in different phases of adopting post-materialistic values by the younger generations having a more post-materialistic view on life.

1.0 - 1.2
1.3 - 1.5
1.6 - 1.8
1.9 - 2.2
2.2 - 2.4
2.5 - 2.7
2.8 - 3.0

Scale 1 (Materialistic society) - 3 (Post-materialistic society)

Post-materialism

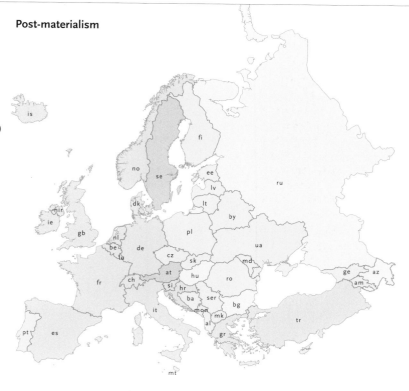

The American political scientist Ronald Inglehart distinguishes between societies with 'post-materialistic' and 'materialistic' attitudes. It is Inglehart's thesis that due to generation replacement, populations of advanced industrial societies have undergone a transformation from a materialistic to a post-materialistic value-orientation. Materialistic means that people emphasize material security or law and order. In a post-materialistic society, people are attracted to freedom and participation in the political process. A post-materialist society places immaterial life-goals such as personal development and self-esteem above material security. The post-materialist thesis is built on two hypotheses. Firstly, the hypothesis of scarcity: the priorities of an individual reflect their socioeconomic environment. One places the greatest subjective value on those things that are in relatively short supply. But the relationship between socioeconomic environment and value priorities is not one of immediate association. For instance: when an adult who was raised in a poor environment suddenly becomes rich, he will not change his materialistic values.

Secondly, there is the socialization hypothesis. A substantial time lag is involved, because basic values reflect the conditions that prevailed during one's pre-adult years, thus the period of socialization. If somebody is raised and socialized in secure circumstances, that is, in a society without scarcity in material goods, he or she will develop a post-materialistic set of values. Evidence for Inglehart's thesis can be found in the sharp partition of Europe along the former Iron Curtain. The western part of Europe went through unprecedented prosperity prevailing from the late 1940s until the early 1970s. This has led to substantial growth in the proportion of post-materialist individuals. In the eastern part of Europe, there was much to be desired. This had lead to a materialistic society.

Post-materialism and welfare

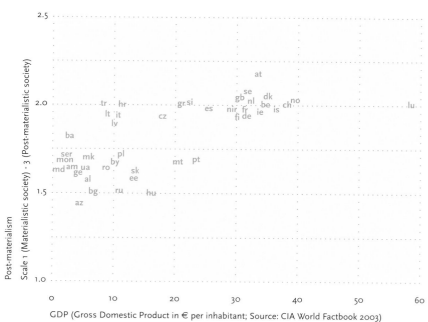

GDP (Gross Domestic Product in € per inhabitant; Source: CIA World Factbook 2003)

Support for democracy

Satisfaction with democracy

The EVS-survey includes the question: On the whole, are you very satisfied, rather satisfied, not very satisfied or not at all satisfied with the way democracy is developing in your country? The option 'rather satisfied' is chosen most often in Europe, however, in total more Europeans appear not satisfied than satisfied: 46% against 54%. Most satisfied with democracy are Luxembourg (83%) and Malta (78%); least satisfied are Russia (7%) and Moldova (10%). In Russia, half of the population appears not at all satisfied. The question is also part of the World Values Surveys which allows a comparison with the USA and other countries. The Americans are considerably more optimistic than the Europeans: 65% is

satisfied. Perhaps surprisingly, the Chinese are among the most optimistic people in the world when it comes to democracy: 88% feels they are on the right track. Russia was also at the bottom of the list in the World Values Studies with a score of 7% satisfied.

European confidence in parliament

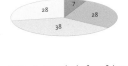

- ■ A great deal of confidence
- ▨ Quite a lot of confidence
- ▧ Not very much confidence
- □ No confidence at all

Weaknesses of democracy

Percentages of people who agree with the statements:

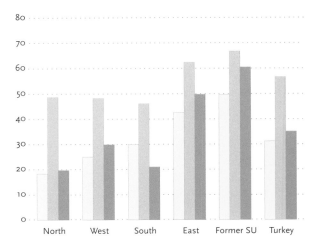

- □ "In democracy the economic system runs badly"
- ▨ "Democracies are indecisive and have too much squabbling"
- ▨ "Democracies aren't good at maintaining order"

Strong leadership

Percentage of people who are in favour of their country being ruled by the army, experts or one 'strong' leader

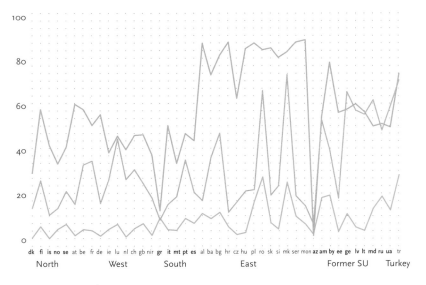

--- Experts (technocracy)
--- A strong leader (dictators)
--- The army

"Democracy may have its problems but is better than any other form of government"

Percentage of agreement

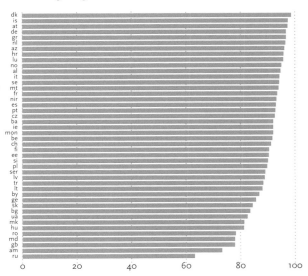

In Turkey, Macedonia, Croatia and Romania more than two thirds of the people think it's a good idea to have a strong leader who does not have to bother with parliament and elections

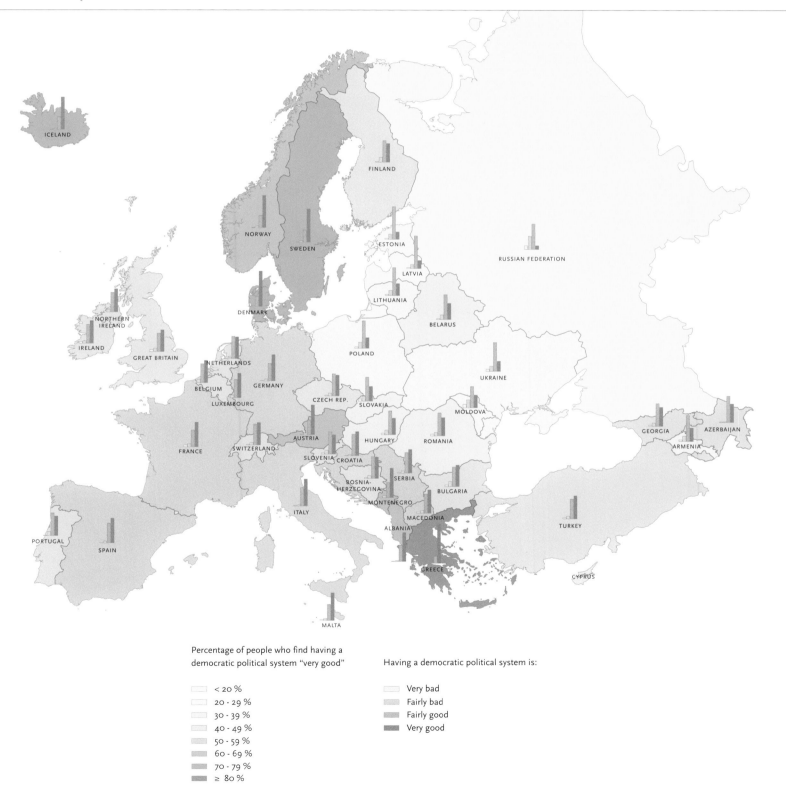

Percentage of people who find having a democratic political system "very good"

	< 20 %
	20 - 29 %
	30 - 39 %
	40 - 49 %
	50 - 59 %
	60 - 69 %
	70 - 79 %
	≥ 80 %

Having a democratic political system is:

	Very bad
	Fairly bad
	Fairly good
	Very good

Today's western society suffers from a decline of civic life, a weakening of social bonds and a loss of social cohesion. At least, that is what many politicians and religious leaders proclaim. The thinning of social connections is in their opinion the distal cause of modern social problems such as a high level of crime, indifference and social isolation. Yet, solidarity and tolerance are still typical European values.

Francis Fukuyama's 'The end of history', Robert Putman's 'Bowling Alone' and Amitai Etzioni's 'The Spirit of Community', all observe a weakening of values and morality. Although these famous social scientists may differ about the causes and the possible solutions of this moral decline, they all depict the future western citizen as a calculating and strongly individualized civilian. A rather gloomy prospect, as they all also agree that a vital, democratic society demands high levels of social trust, cohesion and participation.

The decline of civic engagement is also discussed fiercely in newspapers and parliaments, but suffers noticeably from a blurred terminology. Many definitions and synonyms of the civil society are used: voluntary sector, private government, independent sector,

social economy etc. Perhaps the best scientific definition is made by what the civil society is not: the non-state, non-market and non-private societal domain where voluntary association between citizens is dominant. Examples include non-governmental organisations (NGOs), charities, trade unions, sport clubs, cultural organisations, consumers' bonds, religious groups, environmental parties etc. These organisations are believed to fill the 'gap' between the individual, the state and the market. As such this 'third' sector has also been called the lubricant or cement of society. Engagement in the civil society is thought to have important social spill-over effects: social action creates a more independent citizenry.

Closely linked and often confused with the civil society are social

capital and social trust. Social capital refers to the productive value of civil society and the inclinations that arise from these social networks to do things for each other. Social trust is also strongly associated with civic engagement and vice versa, civic engagement creates social trust. Interpersonal and institutional trust fosters moral bonds, enables cooperation and pro-social behaviour, and decreases 'transaction costs', i.e. when one trusts institutions and people, a reduction of legally binding contracts, legal costs and claims is expected.

Interpersonal and institutional trust are far from constant parameters in Europe. Only ten percent of the Portuguese believe that their fellow countryman can be trusted, whereas a large majority of the Danish think

that their fellow citizens are trustworthy. And where only a quarter of the Greek have confidence in their education and healthcare system, nearly ninety percent of the Austrians have (large) trust in these institutions. Europe is perhaps too diverse to perceive the alleged decline in civil society. But a moral decline is certainly not evident; the permissiveness for cheating or criminal activities is very low.

The evil welfare state
Many causes have been put forward for the apparent loss of community sense. Individualization and seculari-zation are evident explanations, but - perhaps surprisingly - the welfare state has also been blamed. The reasoning is that the welfare state's institutions have taken over the obligations

Public social security expenditure

Public social security expenditure as percentage of the GDP (Gross Domestic Product) in 1996

- ≤ 9 %
- 10 - 14 %
- 15 - 19 %
- 20 - 24 %
- 25 - 29 %
- 30 - 34 %
- ≥ 30 %

Source: World Labour Report 2000 of the International Labour Organization

of support previously located in civil society and family networks. Think for example of care for the elderly and social security. By taking responsibility for social services the welfare state hollowed out and eroded intermediate social structures and as a result commitment, solidarity and trust declined. Additionally, individually felt responsibility is replaced by the idea that the state is responsible for social service. This welfare state pessimism is parried by welfare state optimists who argue that social capital is highest in typical welfare states: the Scandinavian countries. The European Values Study does not provide the ultimate evidence for the pessimists nor for the optimists. High welfare spending does correlate with high levels of social capital, but also has a significant negative effect

on people's informal solidarity towards the needy. Yet, there is no evidence that the latter can be interpreted as a moral 'evil' effect of the welfare state. People do seem to care, but do not worry about the needy groups as they are believed to be well cared for by the welfare institutions.

Tolerance
Closely linked with solidarity and trust is tolerance. Tolerance is generally accepted as a virtue, a common good. Seventy percent of all Europeans want to teach their children tolerance and respect for other people. Sociologists also recognize tolerance as an important value in a free and open society: the more tolerant people are of the rights of others, the more secure are the rights of all. And tolerance undoubtedly promotes a peaceful coexistence

between groups. However, tolerance is a 'slippery' term. In essence, being tolerant means that one accepts the way other people live their lives even when they do not agree with the others' life styles. Tolerance shouldn't be confused with simple indifference to what other people do, but it often is. Intolerance can be widely present within a society, but it is often kept silent and remains untested. Furthermore, tolerance is not an absolute value, there are proper limits to what should be tolerated. This results in the 'paradox of tolerance': a defence of tolerance may require some degree of intolerance. Precisely what the limits of tolerance should be, of course remains a matter of continuous and vigorous debate in society.
Perhaps the best way to measure the tolerance of people well

is to challenge their living environment. The questionnaire of the European Values Study therefore includes the question: Who would you not like to have as neighbours? Drug addicts and heavy drinkers turn out to be the most despised neighbours in all countries, which may be a pragmatic rather than a moral choice as these are exactly the groups one may expect to cause the largest nuisance. Large differentiation among European nations is found in the tolerance towards people with HIV, homosexuals and Jews, with the general trend that the northern and western countries are the most tolerant and Turkey the least.

Social networks

Spending time with other people
Percentage of people who regularly (at least monthly) spend time ...

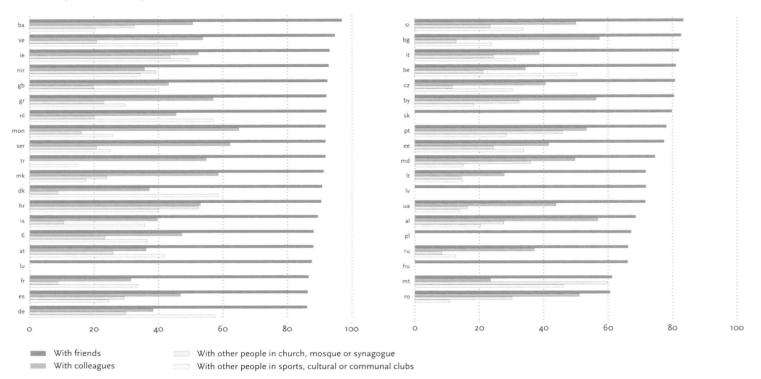

■ With friends
■ With colleagues
▫ With other people in church, mosque or synagogue
▫ With other people in sports, cultural or communal clubs

Percentage of volunteers

Social welfare and community action

Cultural and sports activities

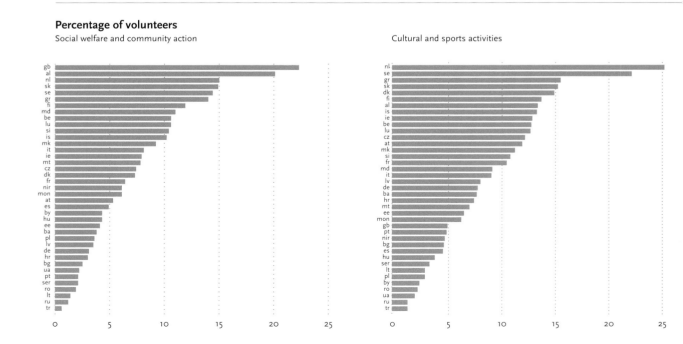

In the Netherlands and Sweden more than half of the inhabitants hold
a membership of some kind of social organization, club or group;
in Russia less than 5% belong to an association

Percentage of people who belong to a voluntary
organization (cultural or political organization,
sports club, peace movement, women groups etc.)

0 - 9 %
10 - 19 %
20 - 29 %
30 - 39 %
40 - 49 %
50 - 59 %
≥ 60 %

Unions and professional organizations

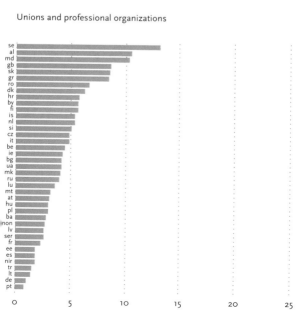

Voluntary work according to age

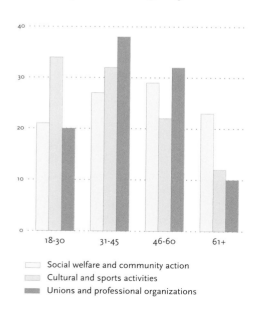

Social welfare and community action
Cultural and sports activities
Unions and professional organizations

Confidence in other people

Percentage of Italians who agree with the statement 'most people can be trusted'

≤ 19 %
20 - 29 %
30 - 39 %
40 - 49 %
50 - 59 %
≥ 60 %

Interpersonal confidence in Italy

Italy is amongst the world's ten largest and strongest economies, but has a marked north-south divide in economic terms. The northern part is highly industrialized and a striking economic success; southern Italy has maintained a strong agricultural character, the unemployment rates are high and welfare is considerably less than in the northern regions. Doubtless, Italy's north-south divide is the result of a long historical process. When Italy was part of the Roman Empire, it had a uniform social and cultural system. The invasion of the South by the Langobards (or Lombards) in the fourth to sixth century brought about a division into a southern "Barbarian" part and the northern Byzantine part, that developed separately until 1861 when Sicily and Naples voted to join the Kingdom of Italy. In his book *Making democracy work: Civic traditions in modern Italy* (1993) the renowned social scientist Robert Putman analyzed the efficacy of the fifteen regional governments in Italy that were installed in 1970. He wanted to reveal why some democratic governments succeed and others fail. Putman concludes that the strength of the civic society has caused the marked difference in political - and also the economical - successes of the North and South, and he links the civil society with levels of trust and cooperation. Putnam argues that the North developed into a society open for modernisation and innovation, while the history of the South was characterised by exploitation and feudalism. The southern vertical tradition produced the lord, vassal, and serf style of relationship, while the horizontal tradition in the North developed into guild, fraternal, and university relationships. In the South, disputes tended to be settled by godfather-like figures; in the North, people tended to form organizations that promoted mutual trust and a team spirit. Putnam's book received much attention as such a strong and convincing link between civil society and economic prosperity was not made before. The figure confirms the assumed north-south divide in levels of trust.

All for one
The North Atlantic Treaty Organization is a military alliance of 26 nations from North America and Europe. These nations have agreed that an armed attack against one of them shall be considered an attack against them all. Nato was established in 1949, predominantly out of concern for the expansion of the USSR, most notably the June 1948 coup in Czechoslovakia, and the blockade of Berlin which started in the same year. Belgium, France, Luxembourg, the Netherlands and the United Kingdom, took the initiative to set up the alliance. Negotiations with the United States and Canada started, and Denmark, Iceland, Italy, Norway and Portugal were invited to participate. In 1952, Greece and Turkey acceded to the treaty. Germany joined in in 1955, and Spain in 1982. After the end of the cold war and the dissolution, in 1991, of the Warsaw pact (the Soviet equivalent to the Nato), the Czech Republic, Hungary and Poland joined in, in 1999. In 2004, another seven East-European countries acceded: Bulgaria, Estonia, Latvia, Lithuania, Romania, Slovakia and Slovenia.

European confidence in Nato

A great deal
Quite a lot
Not very much
None at all

Only 10% of the Portuguese believe that most people can be trusted;
and only 16% of the British have confidence in the press

Confidence in parliament and civil services
Percentage of people who have (much) confidence

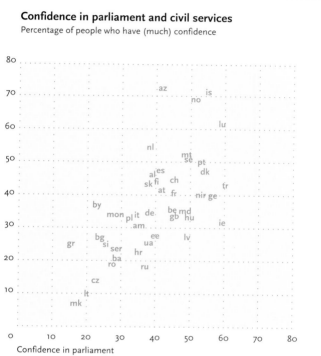

Confidence in parliament

Confidence in other people
Percentage of people who agree with
the statement 'most people can be trusted'

≤ 19 %
20 - 29 %
30 - 39 %
40 - 49 %
50 - 59 %
≥ 60 %

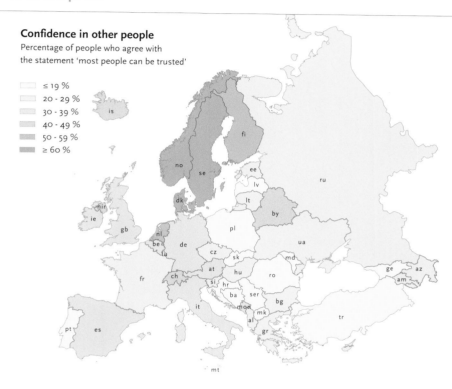

Confidence in the press
Percentage of people who have (much) confidence

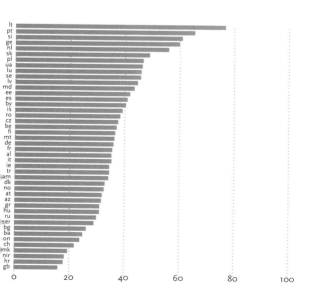

Confidence in the United Nations
Percentage of people who have (much) confidence

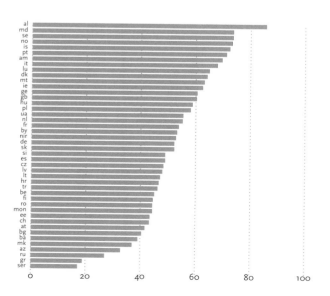

Tolerance

Intolerance: least favourite neighbours

The percentage of people who do not want to live next door to ..

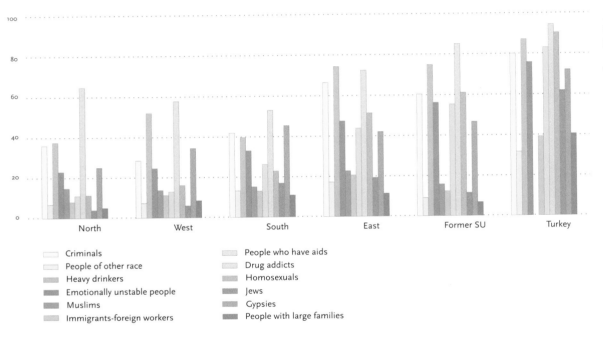

- Criminals
- People of other race
- Heavy drinkers
- Emotionally unstable people
- Muslims
- Immigrants-foreign workers
- People who have aids
- Drug addicts
- Homosexuals
- Jews
- Gypsies
- People with large families

(In)tolerance is hard to measure reliably. Intolerance is often quietly present, and indifference is easily confused with tolerance. Furthermore, tolerance is not an absolute value. Unlike values such as respect or responsibility, there seems to be a threshold of tolerance; there are limits to what a society should be tolerating in order to prevent chaos, offences and conflicts.

In the survey of the European Values Studies, people where asked to indicate who they don't want as a neighbour. In all European regions except Turkey, there is a marked difference between situational and principled tolerance. People appear to base there level of (in)tolerance on the expected amount of nuisance and annoyance. Drug addicts, heavy drinkers and emotionally unstable people are the least favourite neighbours. Intolerance based on ethnic, racial or religious characteristics (people of other race, Jews, Muslims, immigrants) is less common.

Desired action of government on immigration

Percentage of people who find that the government should ...

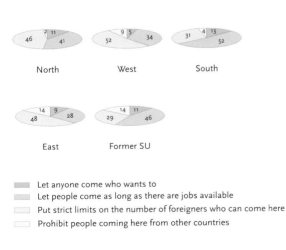

North — 46, 2, 11, 41
West — 52, 9, 5, 34
South — 31, 4, 13, 52
East — 48, 14, 9, 28
Former SU — 29, 14, 11, 46

- Let anyone come who wants to
- Let people come as long as there are jobs available
- Put strict limits on the number of foreigners who can come here
- Prohibit people coming here from other countries

Integration or assimilation

For the greater good of society it is better if immigrants ..

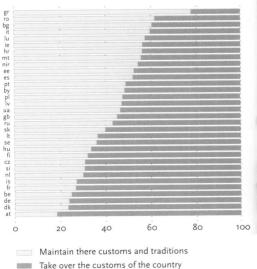

- Maintain there customs and traditions
- Take over the customs of the country

96.6% of the Swedish say they don't object to foreign neighbours;
in Poland this percentage is 71.6; in Turkey only a tiny majority (52.8%)
don't object to living next to foreigners

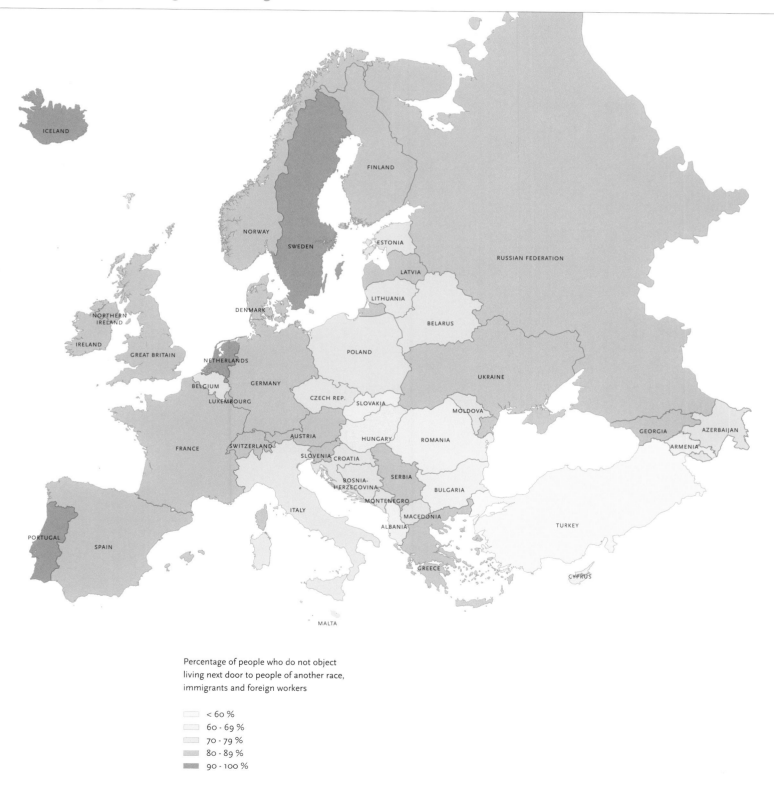

Percentage of people who do not object
living next door to people of another race,
immigrants and foreign workers

< 60 %
60 - 69 %
70 - 79 %
80 - 89 %
90 - 100 %

Solidarity

Solidarity with human kind
Percentage of people who feel (very) much concerned about the living conditions of human kind

- 0 - 9 %
- 10 - 19 %
- 20 - 29 %
- 30 - 39 %
- 40 - 49 %
- 50 - 59 %
- ≥ 60 %

Percentages of people who feel very much concerned about the living conditions of ...

- Family
- Neighbourhood
- Region
- Countrymen
- Europeans

Solidarity with fellow country men
Percentage of people who are (very) concerned about the living conditions of fellow country men according to age

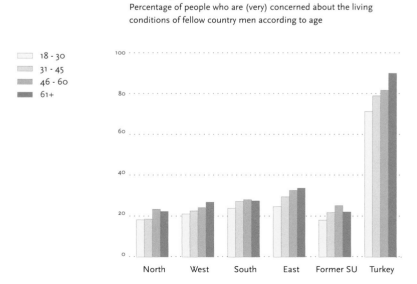

- 18 - 30
- 31 - 45
- 46 - 60
- 61+

Solidarity with fellow Europeans
Percentage of people who are (very) concerned about the living conditions of fellow Europeans according to age

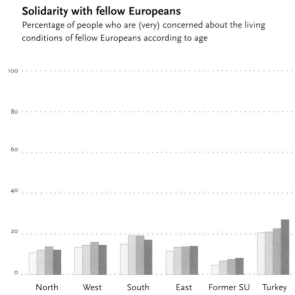

Solidarity with elderly, sick, unemployed and immigrants

Percentage of people who feel (very)
much concerned about the living conditions
of elderly, sick and disabled people,
the unemployed and immigrants

- < 30 %
- 30 - 39 %
- 40 - 49 %
- 50 - 59 %
- 60 - 69 %
- ≥ 70 %

Percentages of people who feel very much
concerned about the living conditions of ...

- Elderly people
- Unemployed
- Immigrants
- Sick and disabled

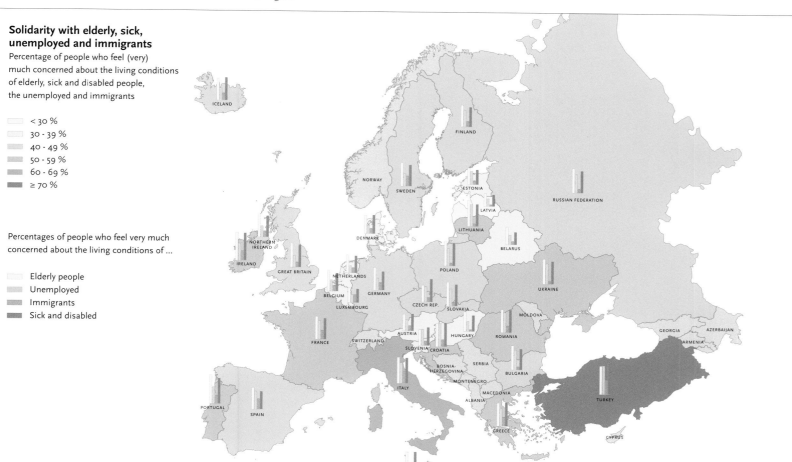

Solidarity with human kind according to income

Percentage of people that are (very) concerned about the
living conditions of human kind

- Low
- Middle
- High

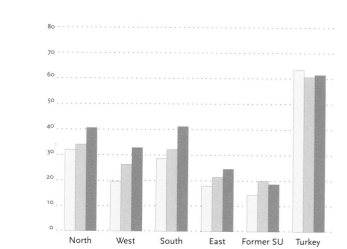

Willingness to improve living conditions for elderly, sick and immigrants

Are you prepared to actually do something to improve the living conditions

Elderly
- Yes
- Maybe
- No

Immigrants
- Yes
- Maybe
- No

Sick and disabled
- Yes
- Maybe
- No

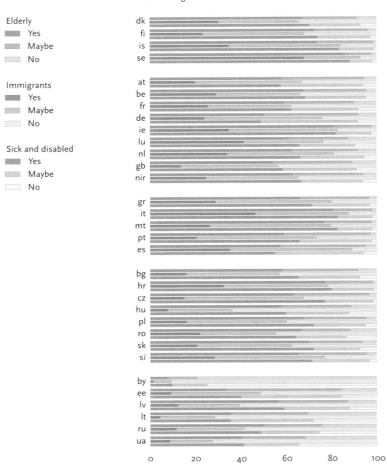

In social science, solidarity is defined as a state of relations between individuals and/or groups which makes it possible that collective interests are served. In daily life, however, solidarity may not be experienced as a good deed towards the collective. People shop for their neighbour who is a bad walker or regularly visit a lonely person simply because it is their neighbour or relative. Yet, although not primarily intended as a benefit to society, these actions do contribute to the well-being of the collective, and as such these actions are a good measure of the degree of solidarity in a social system.

What is immediately clear from the results is that solidarity depends to a large extent on the type of relationship between the well-doer and the recipient: the looser the bond, the lower the intensity. Someone linked by ties of kinship can count on much more support than a neighbour, although the latter are probably much closer in meters. Elderly, sick and disabled people may also count on considerable support. This solidarity is quite logical as seen from a societal viewpoint: we will all grow old and have a large chance of becoming sick at some point in our lives. The European Values Studies also enquired about the reasons why people are willing to help the elderly. Moral duty and sympathy turn out to be the major reasons.

The interest of society and personal interest are only important for a minority. Immigrants meet considerably less solidarity. Mostly because people feel less moral duty towards and sympathy for this group. When people show solidarity with immigrants it is predominantly because they consider it to be in the interest of the greater society.

*"Human solidarity is more and more an individual issue.
It is undergoing a transformation into a contemporary,
more universal but also weaker commitment"*

Paul Dekker
Professor of Civil Society

*Prof. Dr. Paul Dekker is head of
the participation and government
research group at the Social and
Cultural Planning Office of the
Netherlands and a professor of Civil
Society, Globalisation and Sustainable
Development at Globus, an expertise
center of Tilburg University.
Contact: paul.dekker@uvt.nl*

"Social scientists believe that modernization and individualization increase people's solidarity towards persons outside their inner circle: their family, friends, colleagues and neighbours.
The underlying assumption is that the more global orientation of modern citizens results in a higher level of identification and a larger feeling of responsibility.
This theory is confirmed by the high amount of support in modern countries for international relief organisations such as Amnesty, Médicines sans frontières or the Red Cross. In Europe, the sponsorship for these organisations is the highest in typical post-materialistic countries such as Sweden, Iceland and The Netherlands. In the more materialistic southern European countries the support is much lower. Additionally, the national European budgets for development cooperation neatly correlate with levels of modernization.
Therefore one would expect to discern a clear North-South/East difference on the map 'solidarity with human kind' in this atlas, but the contrast is not as apparent as I anticipated. Denmark and Finland show a large level of solidarity, but Greece also. Turkey also had surprising resulting in having a much higher level of solidarity than one may expect from its level of modernization.
Perhaps the line of questioning is partly responsible. Europeans were asked to what extent they felt "concerned about the living conditions of mankind", a formulation that has not quite the same connotation as "solidarity". Furthermore, "mankind" is a rather abstract concept that is difficult to precisely translate in all European languages. And the Turks show very high levels of concern for all types of groups, not specifically for mankind.
Particularly noticeable is the high solidarity with the immediate family throughout Europe. Despite individualization and modernization, the loyalty of people to their direct family remains unattached. This might not be logical, but seems quite natural. Who would understand a mother who cares more for a child in Africa than for one of her own?

Moral duty
Traditionally, global solidarity was strongly embedded in social networks. Donations for Africa were made through the missionary of the church and labour organizations promoted good working conditions and human rights in poor industrializing countries. Today, the importance of these networks is declining, especially in individualizing and secular countries. Human solidarity more and more becomes an individual issue, less restricted by traditional ties, more universal but also thinner, rather resulting in an often superficial commitment. One year someone supports the World Wide Fund for Nature, the next year Amnesty International, and the third year he makes a donation to Unicef. And we see the social paradox that people write to their Plan child in Africa every month, but only notice the absence of their neighbour after she lies dead in her home for half a year. Individualization can result in neglect and even in indifference for people nearby.
Individualized solidarity also makes relief organizations more prone to trends and fashions. Therefore these benevolent organizations depend strongly on the reputation and positive name recognition. Scandals can momentarily ruin an organization, the result being supporters sending the donations to other, more respected, organizations. One can argue that this is a good thing, as it urges an organization towards high standards. However, another consequence is that supporters become less and less involved in the organizations. Instead of raising their voice in the case of discontent, people more easily choose the exit option and go for another organization.
Perhaps the best basis for solidarity is a combination of moral duty and self-interest. It is morally right to help people in need, but it is also wise to support shelter for refugees in their own country, because if we do not they will come to Europe. And one might contribute to the Heart Foundation because of the common good related to more research and better care for the present patients, but it also helps to be aware that this research could one day prolong one's own life as one out of every three people dies from a heart disease.
However, personal interests cannot replace feelings of compassion and moral persuasions as the ultimate foundations of solidarity. Actually, much research shows that people certainly do not act only out of self interest. Moral duty and sympathy for our fellow global citizens are still the main reasons why people support relief organisations and participate in volunteer work. It is important to disclose and elaborate these reasons in social research. Their 'scientific recognition' might help to prevent that terms such as moral obligation and compassion become taboos in the public discourse of our rationalized and secular society."

Reasons for living in need

Pity instead of blame

Some people view poverty as the result of uncontrollable and inescapable factors that are beyond the control of any individual. Others consider it to be the, perhaps unintended, outcome of people's actions and behaviour. The first view is fatalistic, the latter implies that someone or the society can be held responsible for poverty, or may even be blamed for it. Social scientists discern four types of explanations for poverty, combining two dimensions: individual versus society and blame versus fate:

	Individual	Society
Blame	A	C
Fate	B	D

The individual blame type (A) finds that poverty is the result of personal behaviour and shortcomings of the poor themselves. The poor are considered to be lazy, to lack thrift or have loose morals.
The individual fate type (B) believes that poverty is exceptional, and happens to individuals as a matter of just bad luck, God's will or perhaps personal misfortune. Both types deny the possible influence of societal or structural factors.
Opposed to these individual causes of poverty are the societal causes. The social blame type (C) sees poverty as the outcome of processes of social exclusion that are induced and controlled by actions of certain groups and parties in society, who therefore could be blamed for it. The poor are seen as victims of a fundamental injustice: the more powerful groups exclude the weaker groups in their striving towards maximizing their common interests.

Also in the social fate view (D) societal factors and processes are held responsible for poverty, but these processes are regarded as beyond any actors' effective control, that is, as impersonal, objective and unavoidable. The poor are seen as victims of the outcomes of economic market forces, inflation and recession, automation or other technological developments; in short, as victims of broad societal and global developments.
Being ideal-types the four analytically distinguished views do not have to preclude one another in reality. Thus, individuals may have views somewhere in between or tend to regard one of the two dimensions more important than the other.
The four types of explanations for poverty as discussed above, are reflected in people's answers to the European Value Study question 'Why are there people living in

need?'. The possible choices are: because they are unlucky, because of laziness and lack of willpower, because of injustice in our society and it's an inevitable part of modern progress. 'Laziness' represents the individual blame dimension (A), 'unlucky' the individual fate dimension (B); 'injustice' indicates social blame (C), while 'progress' indicates social fate (D).

As can be seen on page 107 the social blame type is dominant in most European countries; the poor are to pity instead of to blame. But variations are high, in Iceland, Ireland and Great Britain, for example, all reasons for poverty score high. Only in a few highly individualized countries poverty is seen as the result of personal behaviour. The Dutch see the poor as unlucky, the Czech, Austrians, Portuguese and North Irish tend to blame them personally.

Reasons for solidarity

The reasons that apply (very) much for Europeans who are willing to help elderly or immigrants

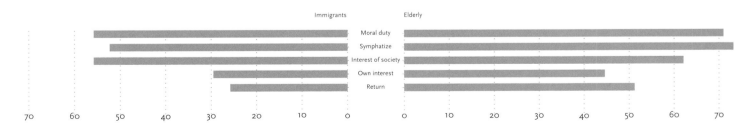

50% of the Maltese think that their fellow countrymen live in need because of laziness and lack of will-power; in Lithuania the same percentage blame the injustice in society

The most important reason why fellow countrymen are in need

- Because they are unlucky
- Because of laziness and lack of willpower
- Because of injustice in our society
- It's an inevitable part of modern progress

Why people live in need

- Because they are unlucky
- Because of laziness and lack of willpower
- Because of injustice in our society
- It's an inevitable part of modern progress

Permissiveness

The myth of moral decline

The process of modernization and individualization is often assumed to be a severe threat to morality. Traditional moral rules are thought to have diminished in favour of a personal morality of 'anything goes'. And indeed on issues like divorce, homosexuality and abortion people no longer rely solely on the judgements and prescriptions of the church. Increasingly, individuals are deciding for themselves, making a personal interpretation and evaluation of the situation at hand. The European Values Studies' survey enquired about the justifiability of 18 moral items and behaviours in an attempt to measure the moral strictness in Europe (see European permissiveness). Homosexuality appears to be the most controversial item. Permissiveness is high in the Netherlands and Sweden, but very low on Malta or in Turkey. The intra-country variations on homosexuality are larger than for other controversial subjects such as euthanasia or abortion. Perhaps to the surprise of many, the results clearly show strict moral rules in all European countries. This applies especially for offences against the law, but even divorce which is the most justifiable action, is accepted only one every two times. And all in all, the 18 items score well below 3 on a scale of 1 through 10. The only justified conclusion is that there is no moral decline in Europe. And as such the rise in criminality can not be explained by the presumed loosening of moral standards. Please note that even a high permissiveness does not mean that respondents have no clear moral standards or that they are likely to adopt the behaviour in question. It only implies that they accept other, perhaps contrasting behaviour.

Permissiveness for homosexuality
Scale 1 (Never justified) - 10 (Always justified)

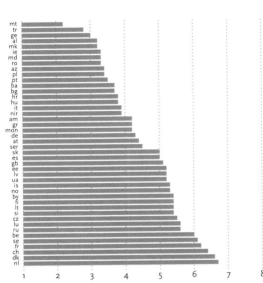

Permissiveness for euthanasia
Scale 1 (Never justified) - 10 (Always justified)

European permissiveness
Scale 1 (Never justified) - 10 (Always justified)

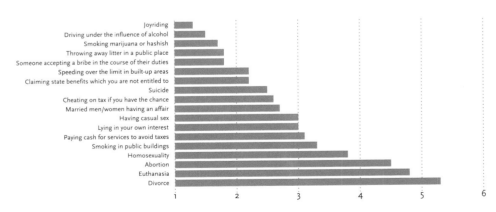

With a score of 7.8 on a scale of 1 (Never justified) to 10 (Always justified) homosexuality is most accepted in the Netherlands;
Hungarians and Azerbaijanis most strongly reject homosexuality, they give a 1.4

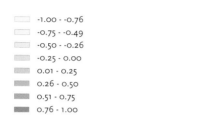

-1.00 - -0.76
-0.75 - -0.49
-0.50 - -0.26
-0.25 - 0.00
0.01 - 0.25
0.26 - 0.50
0.51 - 0.75
0.76 - 1.00

Scale -1 (Never justified) - 1 (Always justified)

The measurement of moral orientations in the European Values Study consists of a long list of items covering a wide variety of moral issues and particular behaviours which an adult living in the twentieth century might confront in his or her life. Respondents were asked to indicate whether or not the behaviours could always be justified, never be justified or something in between. Twenty-four statements were presented, ranging from cheating on taxes and avoiding paying a fare, to political assassinations, homosexuality, and euthanasia.

There appear to be two major areas of permissiveness: civic permissiveness and sexual-ethical permissiveness.

Civic permissiveness refers to behaviours defined by the law as an offence or a crime. It includes the acceptance of deviant behaviours like 'taking free rides on public transport,' 'tax fraud' 'lying in your own interest,' 'accepting a bribe,' and 'political assassinations'. Sexual-ethical permissiveness includes those behaviours which were, and often still are, regarded as sinful according to traditional Christian doctrine, such as 'adultery', 'sex under the legal age of consent,' 'homosexuality,' 'prostitution,' 'euthanasia,' 'divorce,' 'suicide,' and 'killing in self-defence'.

Civic permissiveness

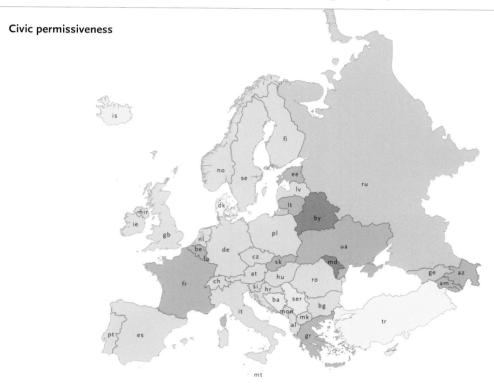

Sexual-ethical permissiveness

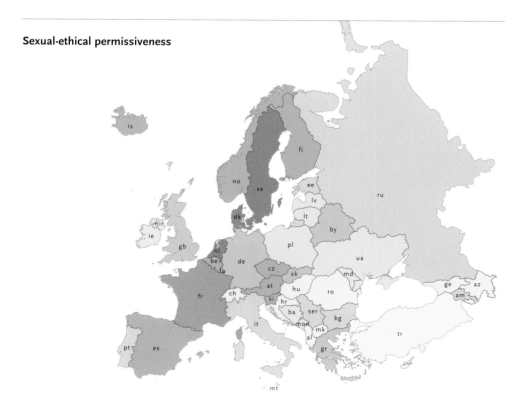

Perceived incidence versus permissiveness

The European Values Study surveys include also a question on perceived incidence of behaviours. Social scientists try to gain more insight in the influence of perceived behaviour on personal permissiveness. Does the permissiveness of an individual towards smoking marijuana or cheating rise when the perceived incidence of these behaviours is high? The answer to this question is not simply yes. People do show herd behaviour and have an inherent drive towards conformity with (unwritten) social rules, but they also in general respect laws. Religious people, in particular, tend to strongly stand for their personal opinions when the perceived behaviour is highly immoral. Furthermore, the perceived incidence may be just what it is: perceived. Some tend to conform to social norms by perceiving that their own behaviour is more common than it actually may be. From the graphs 'Smoking marihuana or hashish' and 'Cheating on taxes' the complex influence between perceived behaviour and permissiveness is evident. Perceived use of drugs does not evidently lead to more use, but also not to less. The same holds true for cheating on taxes. Note, however, that this is a conclusion based on country-level data, not on individual-level data.

Smoking marihuana or hashish

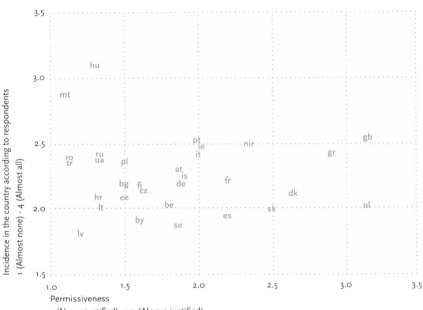

European permissiveness for casual sex according to age
Scale 1 (Never justified) - 10 (Always justified)

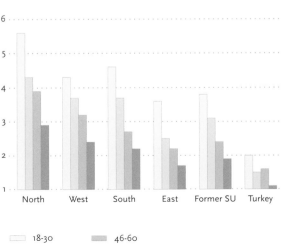

Cheating on taxes

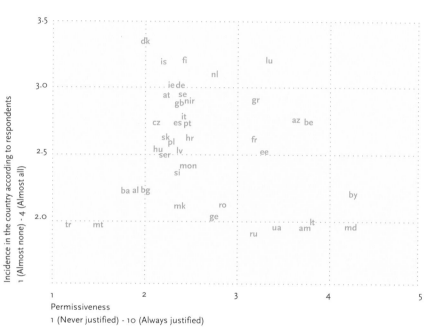

Incidence in the country according to respondents
1 (Almost none) - 4 (Almost all)

Permissiveness
1 (Never justified) - 10 (Always justified)

Frankenstein food

Genetically modified foods - foods
that include DNA of another
organism - are a controversial item.
Vitamin A-enriched rice or a salmon
that grows 400 times as fast as
a natural salmon are considered
by some to be a benefit to society,
while to others this 'superfood' is
Frankenstein food. In 16 of the 42
European countries the European
Values Studies' survey also inquired
about the justifiability of the
genetic manipulation of food stuffs.
Permissiveness is low, from 1.86
in Austria to 3.81 in Belarus on a
scale from 1 (Never justified) to 10
(Always justified). Europeans indeed
view genetically modified food as
Frankenstein food. In Great Britain,
where the term has been invented,
the permissiveness halts at 2.30.

Permissiveness for casual sex
Scale 1 (Never justified) - 10 (Always justified)

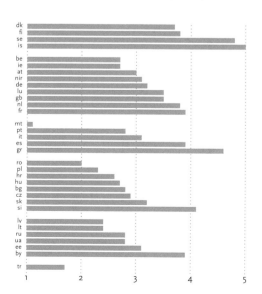

Permissiveness for accepting a bribe
Scale 1 (Never justified) - 10 (Always justified)

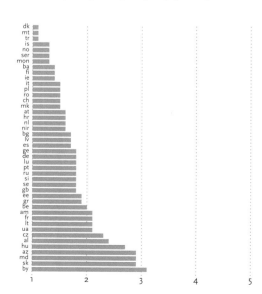

Well-being

Nearly half of the Dutch and Icelanders are very happy with their life. A majority in Romania, Russia, the Ukraine and Bulgaria, however, are unhappy. This could be explained by the large difference in living standards between these countries, but this is apparently not the whole story as the inhabitants of the 'poorest' European country, Albania, put themselves on the happy side of life.

How are you? Although this question may have become more a greeting than an actual sincere inquiry into one's wellbeing, it is no coincidence that we start most of our social contacts by enquiring politely to each others happiness. Well-being or happiness is the individual judgement of the overall quality of one's life, the result of weighing one's mental and health state against one's aspirations and expectations. And as such it is the broadest measure available for assessing the total quality of one's life. By asking 'How are you?' we go straight to the essence of our existence. Well-being, happiness, contentment and satisfaction are often used as synonyms in daily life. However, there are (confusing) differences. Contentment and satisfaction more strongly relate to the degree to which an individual

perceives his material aspirations to be met. One will hardly call oneself unsatisfied when all thinkable earthy endowments are fulfilled, yet one may be very unhappy because of physical or emotional agony. Well-being is the only term used for groups of people or a nation (e.g. the public well-being), often as the antonym of welfare, although generally dwelling conditions and employment changes are also included in well-being.
All in all, there is little consensus of the meaning of these words, even among social scientists.

Born happy
According to the bible there is no reason for happiness here below. Man has been expelled from paradise to this valley of tears, therefore earthly existence is not to

be enjoyed, we are here to chasten our souls. Sigmund Freud saw no reason for happiness either. He perceived happiness as a short-lived orgasmic experience resulting from the release of primitive urges. The more recent psychological literature is only slightly more optimistic. It assumes that aspirations may be followed by achievements, but these lead to new higher aspirations which make enduring happiness impossible. Aspirations may also be followed by disappointment, which leads to lower aspirations. As a consequence periods of happiness and unhappiness oscillate over a lifetime with the average level being neutral.
Luckily, daily practice turns out otherwise. In most European countries happiness is well above

neutral. Satisfaction scores a 6.5 on average, with almost half of the countries above 7.0. What makes all these Europeans happy? Happiness has been said to be a too complex phenomenon to understand, or a too personal one. We are simply born happy or unhappy: the Irish are dead optimistic by nature and the Russians just chronically murky. Others have argued that happiness largely depends on comparison with reference groups. Well-being has no absolute value: improvements will not last, but create more demands and disappointments lead to fewer demands. In other words, we are 'insatiable' when it comes to happiness, but we also 'adjust' to unhappiness. What makes people happy differs from time to time, and from place to place. Nevertheless, Ruut

Human Development Index

⬜	< 0.70
⬜	0.70 - 0.74
⬜	0.75 - 0.78
⬜	0.79 - 0.82
⬜	0.83 - 0.86
⬜	0.87 - 0.90
⬛	0.91 - 0.94
⬛	0.95 - 1.00

Source: United Nations Human Development Report 2001

The Human Development Index of the United Nations is a standard means of measuring well-being. The index was developed in 1990 by the Pakistani economist Mahbub ul Haq. The HDI measures the average achievements in a country in three basic dimensions: A long and healthy life, as measured by life expectancy at birth. Knowledge, as measured by the adult literacy rate and primary, secondary and tertiary gross enrollment ratio. And a decent standard of living, as measured by GDP per capita.

Veenhoven, Professor of sociology in Rotterdam (The Netherlands) and an expert on happiness, has studied the reasons for happiness for many years and discovered by empirical studies many solid correlations between social conditions and well-being.

Wealth

The most evident is that people live happier in rich nations than in poor ones. This relationship between happiness and material comfort is not linear, but follows a concave pattern. Economic growth will add to the average happiness in poor nations, but not in the richer ones. These findings fit the theory that happiness depends very much on the degree to which living conditions fit universal human needs (liveability theory), but as soon as basic needs are satisfied, culturally variable wants become more important. This fits with the comparison theory that teaches that happiness will diminish in the course of time, because of processes like reference and preference drifting. If people satisfy their wants to a higher degree than their reference groups do, they will change eventually their reference groups. If people satisfy their demands to a high degree, they will in time enhance their aspirations level.

Happiness is higher in nations characterized by rule of law, freedom, civil society, cultural diversity and modernity (schooling, technology, urbanization). Together with material comfort, these factors explain almost all differences in happiness across nations. Social equality appears to be unrelated to happiness, as is IQ. Furthermore, happiness is moderately related to social rank in western nations and to social participation. Being embedded in primary networks appears to be crucial to happiness, in particular being married. Surprisingly, the presence of children is unrelated to happiness. Personal character is also important. Happiness is strongly linked to psychological autonomy, i.e. inner control, independence and assertiveness. Happy people are more acceptant of pleasure and more likely to endorse social values such as solidarity, tolerance and love and tend to be less materialistic.

The happy society

Can people be made happy or achieve greater happiness with this knowledge? Can conditions be created that improve everybody's happiness? Welfare is a first and clear means to create happiness, but only to a certain extent. Strengthening of social networks is another option, as is creating freedom and assuring excellent education. Perhaps surprisingly, there is also opposition against policies to optimize happiness. Satisfaction has been said to nurture self-sufficient attitudes, to make people less sensitive to the suffering of others and to demean initiative and creativeness. But social research, including the European Values Study, proves that citizens are the happiest in free, modern democratic nations that respect human rights and have a good education system. Moreover, these happy people tend to be active, educated citizens with independent minds.

Life satisfaction

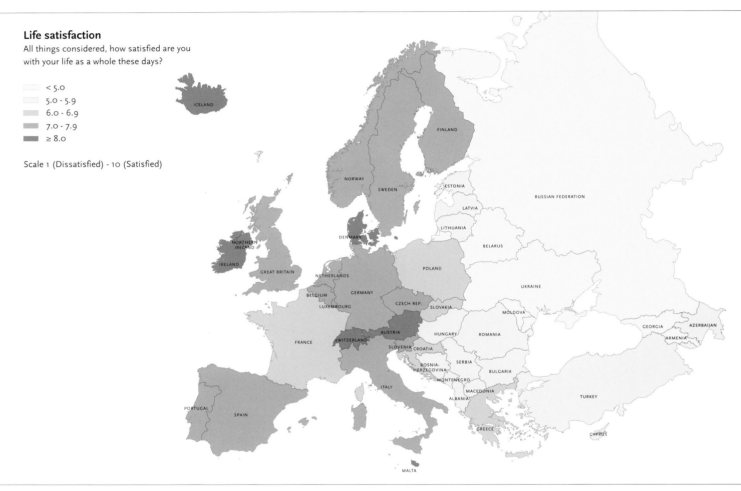

Life satisfaction

All things considered, how satisfied are you with your life as a whole these days?

- ☐ < 5.0
- ☐ 5.0 - 5.9
- ☐ 6.0 - 6.9
- ☐ 7.0 - 7.9
- ■ ≥ 8.0

Scale 1 (Dissatisfied) - 10 (Satisfied)

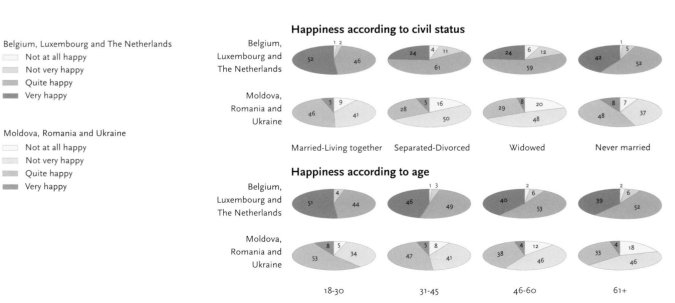

Belgium, Luxembourg and The Netherlands
- ☐ Not at all happy
- ☐ Not very happy
- ☐ Quite happy
- ■ Very happy

Moldova, Romania and Ukraine
- ☐ Not at all happy
- ☐ Not very happy
- ☐ Quite happy
- ■ Very happy

Happiness according to civil status

Belgium, Luxembourg and The Netherlands

Moldova, Romania and Ukraine

Married-Living together   Separated-Divorced   Widowed   Never married

Happiness according to age

Belgium, Luxembourg and The Netherlands

Moldova, Romania and Ukraine

18-30   31-45   46-60   61+

The happiest people in Europe are the Northern Irish: 47.7% are very happy.
The Bulgarians are not so happy: 12.7% are not happy at all

Happiness

Percentage of people who, taking all things
together, are very happy with their life

- 0 - 9
- 10 - 19
- 20 - 29
- 30 - 39
- ≥ 40

Happiness with and without children

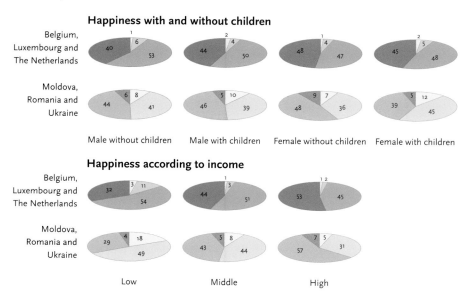

Belgium,
Luxembourg and
The Netherlands

Moldova,
Romania and
Ukraine

Male without children   Male with children   Female without children   Female with children

Happiness according to income

Belgium,
Luxembourg and
The Netherlands

Moldova,
Romania and
Ukraine

Low   Middle   High

**Happiness in Belgium, Luxembourg
and The Netherlands versus Moldova,
Romania and Ukraine**

Belgium, Luxembourg and The Netherlands
are a trio of neighbouring European countries
with a very high level of happiness within the
population. In this figure they are compared
with three other neighbouring countries
that score very low on personal happiness:
Moldova, Romania and The Ukraine. Despite
the large differences in personal happiness,
the variations according to civil status, age,
children and income are quite similar.

Satisfaction versus welfare

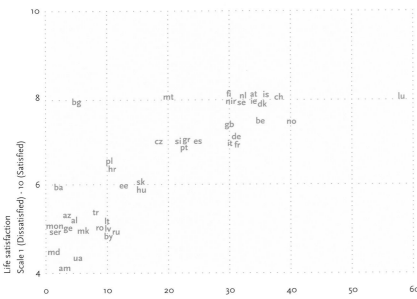

Life satisfaction
Scale 1 (Dissatisfied) - 10 (Satisfied)

GDP (Gross Domestic Product) in € per inhabitant (x 1000)
Source: CIA World Factbook 2003

Happiness and satisfaction according to income

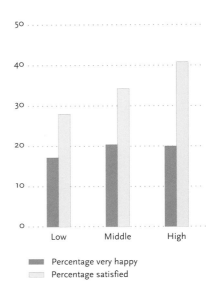

■ Percentage very happy
▫ Percentage satisfied

Happiness versus welfare

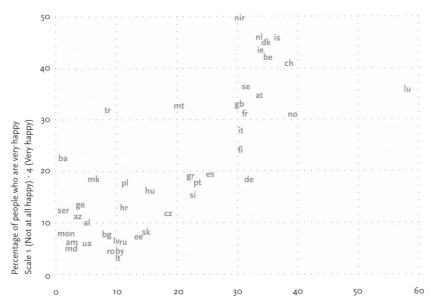

Percentage of people who are very happy
Scale 1 (Not at all happy) - 4 (Very happy)

GDP GDP (Gross Domestic Product) in € per inhabitant (x 1000)
Source: CIA World Factbook 2003

Happiness and satisfaction according to religion

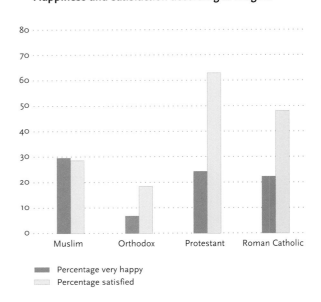

■ Percentage very happy
▫ Percentage satisfied

"Money does provide happiness, but not to the extent that people think, or perhaps hope."

Fred van Raaij
Professor of Economic Psychology

Prof. Dr. W. Fred van Raaij is a professor of Economic Psychology in the Department of Psychology and Society at Tilburg University.
Contact: w.f.vanraaij@uvt.nl

"When I ask someone 'Are you happy?', he or she probably will not give you a reliable account of his or her mental and physical state. People don't want to bother a rather unfamiliar person with their problems and troubles. They hum 'yes' or 'so so', thereby pretending to be happier than they actually are. We like to share our joys and successes, but are hesitant to talk about our hardship and pain. As a result, people generally overestimate the success and happiness of others.

Happiness is in every way a difficult factor to measure scientifically. It is a highly personal and relative concept. To judge happiness, people tend to compare themselves with others. But they tend to choose people that are a little more successful in life or in their career: a colleague, for example, who just got promoted, or the neighbour who has a slightly bigger house or with that friend who found a new love. We do not easily compare ourselves with unhappier people to count our joys, we like to look 'up'. This is an unconscious process which is believed to be functional as it provides us with a drive to be more successful, to achieve. However, it results in being less happy than we can be if we had another reference point.

Today, the most valid way to get a report of people's happiness is by using the Cantrill scale for happiness. People are asked to remember the finest day in their life and mark this day with a 10; accordingly, the worst day ever gets a 0. Then they are asked to scale their current happiness. Still, even such a study is only a 'snapshot' of life. Research has shown that scores are significantly higher on a sunny day, and that a gloomy waiting room for the subjects can drop the scores by a few tenths.

Fleeting joy

People in richer countries are evidently happier than those in poorer nations. Especially, the inhabitants of small, high-welfare states are happy. This proves that money does provide some happiness. But money does not provide joy to the extent that people assume, or perhaps hope. People tend to think that they will only be completely happy after the next promotion or after buying that larger house. In fact, they do become happier, but this positive effect soon disappears. Because before long, they start to compare themselves with their new colleagues or suddenly realize that the new house is one of the smallest in their new neighbourhood.

Scientists have actually measured and proven this effect. Economist Bernard van Praag, for example, asked people what income would satisfy them, and repeated this question a few times in the following years. The people indicated to need more and more money to be satisfied. The salary that they had once thought would make them happy at the start of their career was not sufficient once they actually received the originally desired salary. It is rather unfortunate that people think that they will become happy from material stuff, and in fact it is also quite illogical. Because, when you ask someone what makes him or her happy, a good relationship and a nice family are top priorities. In second place comes a pleasant and meaningful job. Possessions and money only rank third. Indeed, couples are happier than singles, but it is tricky to conclude that marriage makes them happy. Perhaps, people with a more cheerful disposition who easily find a life partner are happier, whereas the worriers stay single.

Anyhow, true happiness does not come easily. An evening of alcohol abuse or sex can provide ecstasy, but it is short-lived. In fact, these types of happiness resemble an addiction, where greater quantity and quality are needed to sustain the original high. Lasting happiness only seems to come from lengthy efforts: ten years of marriage, your child's graduation or the completion of a novel or dissertation. The process of getting there may not always be pleasant, but the resulting happiness is long lasting. This is probably so because one has proven their talents and went through hardship to get there. Yet, in our modern hedonistic society, many people choose for the short, fleeting joys to which so many advertisements and commercials tempt. One could argue that someone would be much happier after four years of studying than four years of partying, however few would believe this."

In control of your life

Life is what you make it

The European Values Study confirms a well-known notion in psychology that people are more happy when they feel they have some control over the way their life turns out. In psychology, this feeling of being in control is known as the locus of control, and is considered an important aspect of one's personality.

Individuals with an external locus of control believe that life is guided by faith, luck or other external circumstances. Their own behaviour doesn't matter very much; rewards in life are considered outside of their control. On the contrary, individuals with a strong internal locus of control believe

that life is steered by their own personal decisions and efforts: life is what you make it. The concept of a locus of control was developed by psychologist Julian Rotter in the 1960's. Psychological research has found that people with a more internal locus of control are generally better off. For example, they tend to have the better paid jobs. However, overly internal people, particularly those lacking confidence, may be neurotic, anxious and depressed. And many people with an external locus of control live happy lives. The good news is that locus of control appears largely learned and can be changed.

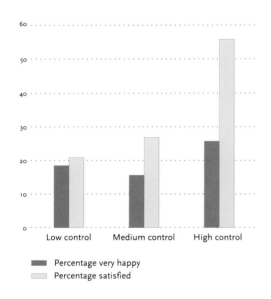

Happiness, satisfaction and control

■ Percentage very happy
□ Percentage satisfied

What makes one happier

Would be ....
□ A good thing
▨ Don't mind
■ A bad thing

Less emphasis on money and material possessions

North	West	South	East	Former SU	Turkey
20 / 14 / 66	20 / 19 / 61	17 / 10 / 73	28 / 15 / 57	41 / 13 / 47	12 / 18 / 70

Decrease in the importance of work in our lives

| 49 / 14 / 36 | 33 / 18 / 48 | 52 / 15 / 33 | 74 / 17 / 9 | 72 / 17 / 11 | 62 / 26 / 11 |

More emphasis on the development of technology

| 27 / 25 / 48 | 24 / 15 / 61 | 24 / 14 / 62 | 15 / 8 / 78 | 9 / 3 / 87 | 7 / 4 / 90 |

Greater emphasis on the development of the individual

| 6 / 3 / 91 | 11 / 3 / 86 | 7 / 3 / 90 | 10 / 4 / 86 | 6 / 2 / 92 | 4 / 1 / 95 |

More emphasis on family life

| 9 / 2 / 89 | 8 / 2 / 90 | 8 / 2 / 90 | 5 / 2 / 94 | 6 / 1 / 93 | 2 / 1 / 97 |

A simple and more natural lifestyle

| 14 / 4 / 82 | 14 / 7 / 79 | 9 / 2 / 89 | 10 / 5 / 85 | 22 / 18 / 61 | 17 / 16 / 67 |

North West South East Former SU Turkey

The people of Iceland feel they have high control over the way their lives turns out; Turks report the lowest level of control within Europe

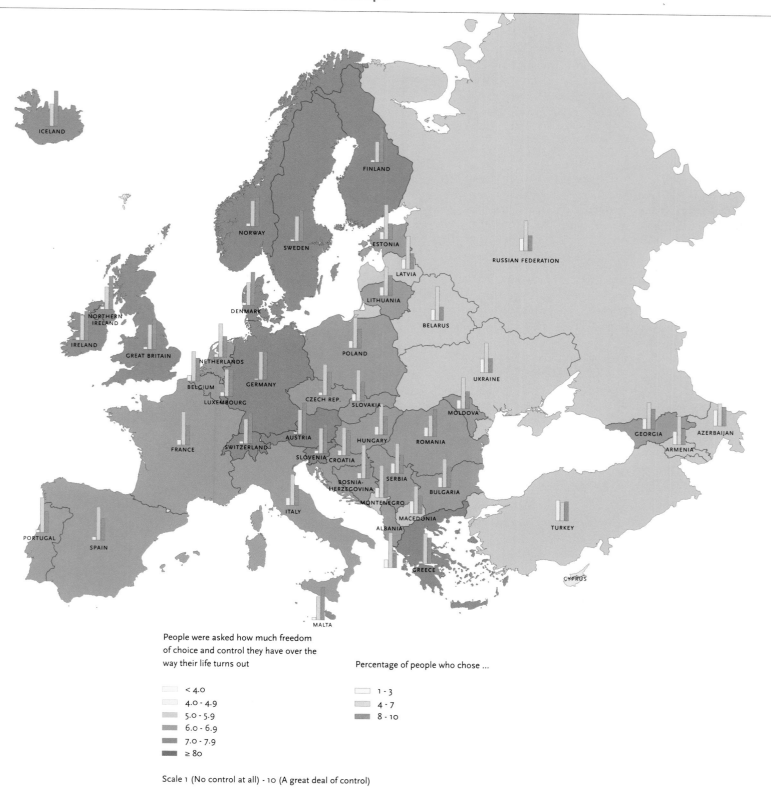

People were asked how much freedom
of choice and control they have over the
way their life turns out

Percentage of people who chose ...

☐ < 4.0	☐ 1 - 3
☐ 4.0 - 4.9	☐ 4 - 7
☐ 5.0 - 5.9	☐ 8 - 10
☐ 6.0 - 6.9	
☐ 7.0 - 7.9	
☐ ≥ 80	

Scale 1 (No control at all) - 10 (A great deal of control)

Epilogue

Happy and satisfied

In the seven thematic chapters of this atlas, a selection of the data from the most recent European Values Study surveys has been presented. From this data, it is clear that a substantial majority of Europeans applaud unification, but that only a few actually feel European. When it comes to family values, Europeans appear surprisingly conservative. 'Married-with-children' is still the preferred lifestyle for a vast majority. European women working outside their home are generally well-accepted, but only as long as their children come first. And although Europeans do appreciate an interesting and meaningful job, good pay is most important. Church attendance is declining everywhere, but a vast majority considers themselves religious and believes in some kind of God. In fact, the European continent is not as secularized as it may seem at first sight. Furthermore, the presumed East-West divide is blurring. The young democracies in the East more and more resemble the 'old' Western ones. Despite all stories on moral decline, solidarity and tolerance are still highly valued throughout Europe. And although daily practice may perhaps indicate otherwise, Europeans en masse reject illegal activities such as driving over the speed limit or cheating on taxes. Finally, Europeans are on average happy and satisfied, especially those in the more wealthy countries.

Europe's values map

But what general conclusions may be drawn from the comprehensive set of EVS-data on values and attitudes? What underlying patterns can be discerned in Europe's moral? Where is Europe heading? Social scientists Jacques Hagenaars, Loek Halman and Guy Moors of Tilburg University condensed all EVS-data into one plot (see Europe's value map), a cultural map of Europe in which each country is represented by a single point. The map immediately reveals that Europe is not a homogeneous part of the world, the countries are scattered all over.

The only clear predictor of a country's position on the cultural map appears to be its economic development. The wealthier a country is, the more it shifts to the right, representing high levels of personal autonomy. Although there are some exceptions (notably Finland and Hungary), economic prosperity and the corresponding level of social security appear to steer values in this direction. The question is, however, which is the prevailing direction of causality. Does economic welfare change the values, or do changing values bring along economic prosperity? A classical chicken-and-egg problem. The high individualism that characterizes these economically advanced countries should not be interpreted in terms of egoism, narcissism, hedonism or even ethical relativism; this type of individualism does not lack a communal spirit, but is socially committed. The wealthier Northern and Western countries are the most lenient in personal sexual matters. Women with careers are widespread and accepted. Tolerance towards people of different ethnic background or displaying deviant behaviour is high. Children and marriage are not regarded as an absolute necessity and organizations are less authoritarian.

The strong link between personal autonomy and wealth concurs with existing social theories on individualization and increasing post-materialism and post-modernization. In short, these theories state that the unprecedented economic prosperity of advanced industrial (Western) societies gradually brought a shift from materialism to post-materialism. Economic and physical security allows people to give priority to values related to quality of life issues, self-realisation, environmentalism and social concerns such as minority rights, fair trade, gender equality and the like. Post-modernization theory originates in Abraham Maslow's classic hierarchy of needs. Psychologist Maslow argued that human beings assign clear, hierarchical priorities to their individual needs. Only when a person has reached a particular level in his own needs pyramid, the need to achieve the next higher level is aroused. The base of the pyramid is formed by physical needs, such as food and shelter. The following levels are formed by a hierarchy of needs starting with the need for safety and security, followed by a desire to be loved and have sense of belonging, then an aspiration respect, and finally self-actualization. Post-modernization theory can be seen as Maslow's theory applied to the evolution of societies. Only when certain basic societal needs are fulfilled, will a society's population strive for 'higher' values such as personal autonomy and individual freedom.

The only clear predictor of a country's position on the cultural map
appears to be its economic development

Europe's values map

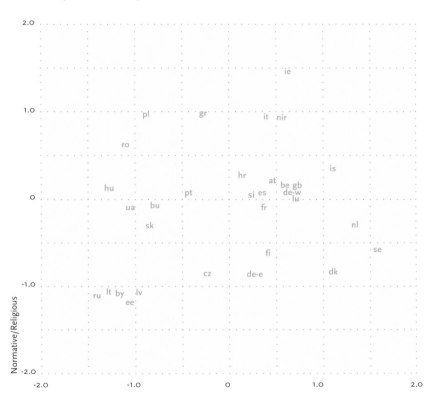

Autonomy/Socio-liberalism
N.B. Germany is divided into de-e and de-w (former East-Germany and former West-Germany)

Each country's value set is represented by a point in this two dimensional value space. The two fundamental value dimensions have been calculated by statistical analysis from about forty items in the EVS questionnaires (e.g. work ethos, solidarity, religiosity, post-materialism). The first dimension is called the autonomous/social-liberal dimension and reflects personal autonomy and individual freedom. Countries that rank high on this dimension favour personal autonomy over authority. They are permissive towards personal sexual matters and regard children and marriage as an option, not as a necessity. Emancipation is high as is tolerance towards people of different ethnic background or showing deviant behaviour. The second dimension, which is statistically independent from the first, combines a number of normative issues. Individuals and countries that score negative on this dimension maintain strict moral standards, they highly value societal norms and institutions and stress solidarity. Civil morality is high since self-interest and illegal behaviour is rejected. Abortion is disapproved of and marriage and the intrinsic meaning of work are important. High positive values reflect a highly secular society.

Source: Exploring Europe's basic values map, Jacques Hagenaars, Loek Halman & Guy Moors in The cultural diversity of European unity, European Values Studies Vol. VI, Brill Leiden-Boston 2003, p. 23

The Southern European countries are predominantly found in the upper part of the map that represents strict moral standards. Citizens of Southern Europe put a high value on societal norms and institutions, and stress solidarity. Civil morality is high since self-interest and illegal behaviour are rejected. Abortion is disapproved of and marriage and the intrinsic meaning of work are important. Not surprisingly, many of these countries' citizens are religious.

A country's position on the vertical, normative-religious dimension is not easily explained. Economically more developed countries such as Italy and Denmark score very differently. And historically and culturally very different countries such as the Ukraine and the United Kingdom resemble each other. The order is also not simply explained by level of religiosity, although Catholic societies seem stricter than Protestant and Orthodox countries. One cannot but conclude that the order reflects a mix of cultural and political heritages and religious tradition.

Despite the common Christian tradition, European unity seems to be a unity of diversity. There appear significant differences between Europe's societies that have to do not only with different levels of economic development, but also with varieties in cultural heritages, languages, religious and ideological traditions and differences in political and educational systems. Value orientations appear dependent upon specific national contexts and a nation's historical development.

East versus West

The final breakdown of the Soviet Union in 1991 was an historical event for Europe. The Iron Curtain that had separated the 'communist' East from the 'capitalist' West for decades was finally removed. The velvet revolutions carried most Eastern countries into multi-party democracies in a matter of months. The socio-economic orientation towards a free market economy took considerably more time, and in some cases, has not been fully completed.

A pivotal question after the fall of the iron curtain is if the 'value-divide' between East and West will disappear. Now that democracy and capitalism have set ground in the post-communistic countries, will the East-West divide start to blur? There are indeed indications that the change towards a market economy 'pushes' values towards more Western norms, but according to the European Values Study value differences remain. The former communist countries are mainly found in the lower-left quadrant of the values map. Indicating that they are more conservative than the Western and Northern countries. These nations also favour a much stronger role for the state in directing the economy and ensuring the social safety net than their counterparts in Western Europe. And they are less prone to do voluntary work, while interpersonal confidence is rather low, as is their overall life satisfaction. And EVS also reveals the citizens in the East feel less European.

However, speaking about the East does not do justice to the sometimes wide cultural differences that exist in this region. Belarus and Georgia, for example, can hardly be compared with the more Nordic-oriented Estonia or western-oriented Slovenia in terms of history or cultural heritage. The differences among the former communistic countries are large. Seven former Soviet states have fully converted to a market economy and have joined the European Union: Poland, Estonia, Latvia, Lithuania, Czech Republic, Hungary, Slovenia, Slovakia. Romania, Bulgaria and Croatia are candidate countries. But others Eastern countries such as Ukraine, Moldova, Russia or Azerbaijan may never apply for membership as their cultural and historical roots have little in common with the other members.

As said before, economic development pushes the Eastern countries in the direction of the others. And also a country's geographic and cultural proximity to the West seems to result in more 'western' values. The Czech Republic and Poland far more resemble Austria or France, than Latvia or Russia. Will the differences between East and West become smaller? Will the European countries grow towards each other in terms of values? To answer these questions the European Values Study is in fact too young. There have been three 'waves' of surveys (not all countries were included in all surveys), in 1981, 1990 and 1999/2000. Twenty years may seem like a long time, but it is generally considered too small to investigate value changes. For Western-European countries (which are well-represented in all three EVS-waves) a steady increase in socio-liberal values can be seen. If this trend continues, these countries will all establish a high level of autonomy and socio-liberalism. There has also been an increase in normative/religious values from 1981-1990. However, this trend did not persist in the 1999/2000 wave. Furthermore, cultural changes most often take place by generational shifts rather then through people changing their views in a fundamental way. In each new 'wave', the oldest and most likely conservative generation is replaced by a younger generation with usually more modern values. As far as 'autonomy and social liberal' values are concerned, a small but steady increase is observed for each younger generation between 1981 and 2000. An interesting result, however, is that the continuous upward trend over the generation towards more autonomy starting from the post-war birth cohort 1940-1945 appears to slow down. In terms of normative/religious values no clear rise or fall can be seen over the various generations.

Men versus women

Opinions about the appropriate roles of men and women in society have changed considerably over the past fifty years. Virtually all over Europe, the support for a rigid division of labour between husbands and wives is diminishing. Married women who work outside their home have been rapidly accepted, and men are more and more expected to become involved in traditional female activities such as raising children and household chores.

Men and women are increasingly supposed to engage in activities that traditionally belonged to the opposite gender. Even more so, it is believed that women should participate on the labour market. Equally, it is not only accepted that men are involved in child care, they are also expected to contribute to household chores. Traditional norms are gradually replaced by new, modern norms and there is an increasing commitment to the principle of equal rights and opportunities for men and women. This sex-role revolution occurred in almost all western societies, but the timing and speed of the trends differs across countries. In contemporary Europe, the most liberal opinions about sex-roles are found in the Scandinavian countries and the Netherlands. Among the more conservative opinions regarding traditional gender roles are Malta, Poland and Turkey. Like other value changes, the sex-role revolution has been explained from two theoretical perspectives: a cultural and an economic viewpoint. The cultural perspective links the sex-role revolution to other major value changes in society. Equal rights and opportunities for men and women are believed to be part or a result of individualization and secularization. And indeed it is found that church attendance correlates with more traditional sex-role attitudes. When a ranking has to be made, Protestants are more liberal than Catholics, followed by the Orthodox and supporters of other religions (including Muslims).

The second explanation is economic. Changing sex-role attitudes are believed to be the result of changes in women's employment. The expansion of the service sector resulted in a considerable growth of traditionally female occupations and this pulled more and more (married) women into the labour market. This theory is also confirmed by the EVS-data. Countries with a high participation rate of women rank among the more liberal in terms of sex-role attitudes. However, within countries there can be a substantial difference. In Sweden, for example, women are much more liberal than men, while in traditional Italy, the opinions of men and women are more in agreement.

School enrolment also has a strong liberalizing effect on sex-role attitudes, although the effect is more consistent for women than for men. This corroborates the idea that students in higher education are more liberal on all sorts of issues.

Although individual employment, church attendance and a high level of education correlate with sex-role attitudes, these characteristics can only explain a small part of the variance in sex-role attitudes. The national context appears to be a rather good proxy for explaining the differences and similarities between men and women in the values they cherish. It is, however, not clear to which national characteristics the country label refers. Traditions, institutions, behavioural patterns or perhaps socialization patterns?

Relative importance of life domains

Percentage of people indicating their family, work, friends, religion or leisure time as very important in their life

Family
Work
Friends
Leisure time
Religion

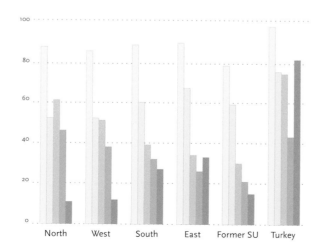

Europe versus the world

The most important conclusion of the European Values Study may be that Europe is not a homogenous part of the world in terms of its values. But how does Europe compare with the rest of the world? To find an answer to this question we need to look beyond the European Values Study and consult the World Values Survey which also includes nearly forty non-European countries, among which the United States, Japan, China, Mexico, Brazil and Nigeria are included. On the basis of this data a world values map can be drawn which allows an analysis of Europe's position in the world (see World's values map).

Again, wealth appears to be the only clear predictor of a country's position on the cultural map. Economic development moves countries to the upper-right side of the chart, the part that corresponds with high levels of modernism and post-modernism. The majority of Western nations are found to be within the same quadrant, indicating a secular worldview in which authority is legitimated by rational-legal norms and an emphasis on economic accumulation and individual achievement. The Eastern European countries are now predominantly found in the upper-left side of the chart, the section that represents societies emphasizing survival values: hard work and economic and physical security. The further to the left, the higher the insecurity in these countries, resulting also in low levels of interpersonal trust, intolerance towards out-groups and low support for gender equality. These societies also show high faith in science and technology, relatively low support for environmental activism, and relatively high backing for authoritarian government.

Apart from a large influence of economic development, the map provides strong evidence for the persistence of cultural traditions. The difference in GDP per capita between Poland and Estonia, for example, is small. Also geographically, they are not far apart. Yet, in the cultural map of the world, it is evident that the Poles are much more traditional than the Estonian people. Additionally, it is interesting that the historically Protestant societies are found more to the right than the historically Catholic societies. And the more family-oriented southern European countries (France, Greece, Italy and Spain) also group together. History and culture thus leave their traces on the world's values map.

Where to?

To Europeans, the United States always has been regarded as a kind of societal reflection of the future. California's slogan 'the future happens here first' is widely assumed to be true, although many do not heartily welcome this future. American society is by many Europeans perceived as violent and rather impersonal. But, according to the world's values map, the US is not the prototype of cultural modernization; it has a much more traditional value system than any other advanced industrial society. Modernization is not synonymous with Americanization.

The US is also clearly not 'European'; it is not found amid the European societies, but takes a position on Europe's cultural boundaries. From the European nations, the US most closely resembles Austria, but it is closer to other young societies such as Australia, Canada or New Zealand.

Globally, Japan, Germany, Sweden and Norway appear the most modern societies, they are the least attached to religious or cultural traditions. The reasons behind this vary. Japan represents the relatively secular-bureaucratic Confucian tradition. All countries experienced the secularizing impact of affluent post-industrial societies, which especially in the case of Germany, Sweden and Norway is accompanied by a well-developed welfare state.

When it comes to self-development and personal autonomy, Sweden and the Netherlands score the highest. These societies are the most tolerant towards deviant (sexual) behaviour, meanings or attitudes. Economic progress explains their positions to a large extent, both are among the wealthiest countries in the world. These countries also resemble each other in having an advanced welfare state and in being relatively small in terms of population.

Both the values map of Europe and the world, indicate that the Scandinavian people and perhaps also the Dutch are on the cutting edge of cultural change. They have advanced the furthest in the direction of modernization and post-materialism. When sociological theories are correct, and their trajectories will be followed by others, Europeans do not have to look over the ocean, but to the North to see their future.

The US is not the prototype of cultural modernization;
the Scandinavian people are on the cutting edge of cultural change

World's values map

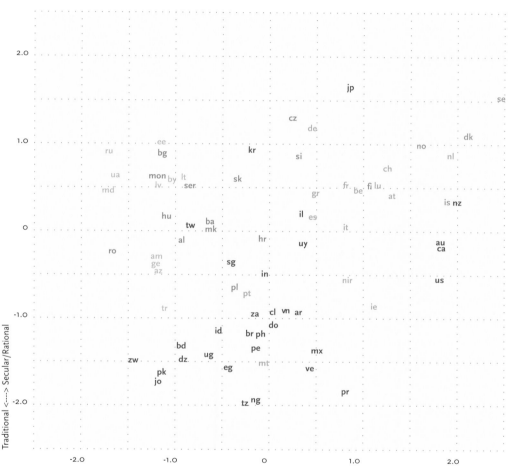

——— North
——— West
——— South
——— East
——— Former SU
——— Turkey
——— Non-European countries

In this global value map, based on the results of the World Values Survey, each country is characterized by its level of modernization (vertical axis) and post modernization (horizontal axis). Modernization is characterized as economic development and progress through industrialization and is associated by urbanization and mass communication. Post-modernization represents a later stage of societal development that emphasizes human choice and self-expression. Please note that these dimensions differ from those in Europe's values map.

A negative score on the modernization dimension represents traditional views and values: obedience to traditional authority, usually religious authority, and adherence to family and communal obligations. A positive score relates to a secular worldview in which authority is legitimated by rational-legal norms, linked with emphasis on economic accumulation and individual achievement. Societies that score low on the post-modernization dimension emphasize survival values: hard work and economic and physical security. These society's are generally characterized by high insecurity and low levels of interpersonal trust, intolerance towards out-groups and low support for gender equality. A high score presents high self-expression values: equal rights for women, sexual and ethnic minorities and self-development.

Source: Human beliefs and values, a cross-cultural sourcebook based on the 1999-2002 values surveys, R. Inglehart, M. Basáñez, J. Díez-Medrano, L. Halman & R. Luijkx Eds. Siglo XXI Editores, Mexico (2004)

Traditional <—-> Secular/Rational

Survival <—-> Self-expression

Country abbreviations for non-European countries:

dz	Algeria	id	Indonesia	ph	Philippines
ar	Argentina	il	Israel	pr	Puerto Rico
au	Australia	jp	Japan	sg	Singapore
bd	Bangladesh	jo	Jordan	za	South Africa
br	Brazil	kr	Korea	tz	Tanzania
ca	Canada	mk	Macedonia	ug	Uganda
cl	Chile	mx	Mexico	us	United States of America
tw	Taiwan	nz	New Zealand	uy	Uruguay
do	Dominican Republic	ng	Nigeria	ve	Venezuela
eg	Egypt	pk	Pakistan	vn	Vietnam
in	India	pe	Peru	zw	Zimbabwe

Acknowledgment

The data in this atlas is based on the most recent surveys in all countries in Europe, conducted within the framework of the European Values Study and the World Values Surveys. These values projects are large-scale, cross-national, and longitudinal survey research programs on basic human values, initiated by the European Value Systems Study Group (EVSSG) in the late 1970s. The initial researchers aimed at exploring the moral and social values underlying European social and political institutions and governing conduct. Questions were raised such as: Do Europeans share common values? Are values changing in Europe and, if so, in what directions? Do Christian values continue to permeate European life and culture? Is a coherent alternative meaning system replacing that of Christianity? These questions and issues are still relevant today.

To answer these questions, a survey was planned in all member states of the European Community. This survey was fielded in 1981 and interviews were held in ten countries. The research project aroused interest in Northern Europe, North and South America, the Middle and Far East, Australia and South Africa, where affiliated groups were set up to administer the same questionnaire. Agreements were negotiated with regard to the exchange of data for intercontinental and inter-cultural comparisons. As a result a unique data set became available in the 1980s, covering 26 nations.

In order to explore value changes, successive waves of surveys were carried out in 1990-1991 by the European Values Study, and in 1995-1996 by the World Values Surveys. Each successive wave covered a broader range of societies than the previous one. Analyses of each successive wave yielded that certain questions tapped theoretically interesting and substantially important concepts while others appeared of little value. This resulted in a replication of the useful items in new waves while redundant items were dropped, making room for new items and questions.

For each wave a master questionnaire was produced in the English language, which was translated into the national languages. In all countries, the surveys were performed through face-to-face interviews among samples of all adult citizens aged 18 years and older. No upper age limit was imposed. Guidelines for the surveys were provided by the coordinating organisation at Tilburg University. Detailed information on the translation of the questionnaire, the sampling procedures, fieldwork, weighting, national codes etc. can be found in the sourcebook of the 1999/2000 European Values Study Surveys (Halman, 2001), the EVS website (www.europeanvalues.nl) and the website of the World Values Surveys (www.worldvaluessurvey.org).

The 1999/2000 EVS surveys were coordinated from Tilburg University in close collaboration with *Zentralarchiv für Empirische Sozialforschung* in Cologne (ZA) and the Netherlands Institute for Scientific Information Services (NIWI) in Amsterdam. All national datasets that were collected within the framework of EVS were combined into one integrated dataset and a master codebook based on the national datasets, the national questionnaires and master questionnaire were documented and released on CD-Rom ("EVS 1999/2000") containing 33 national datasets, the integrated dataset and all relevant documentation (Luijkx, Brislinger & Zenk-Moeltgen, 2003). The data of the other European countries included in this atlas was collected within the framework of the WVS. This data were cleaned and combined into one integrated dataset by JD Systems in Madrid. Both EVS and WVS data was combined by JD Systems that, in close collaboration with Tilburg University, also produced a CD-Rom containing not only the integrated dataset but also all relevant documentation. This CD-ROM is included in the sourcebook on all 1999-2002 surveys (Inglehart, Basáñez, Díez-Medrano, Halman & Luijkx, 2004).

All data is available to a broader audience and can be obtained through the national data archives or directly from Zentralarchiv in Cologne: www.gesis.org/za.

Maps

The maps presented in this atlas are not entirely geographically accurate. In order to include all European countries in a way that properly distinguish the nuances of each country the maps have been slightly adjusted, which may yield a geographically distorted picture of Europe. For example, Malta is larger than in reality, Iceland is closer to the main land than in reality, and details of the coastal line of Norway are left out.

On the maps, the differences in value orientations, attitudes and opinions etc. are indicated by a variety of colours. The colour grey is used (i.e. Cyprus) when no or no comparable data was available, as a consequence of having not asked the specific question or in case a question was differently phrased or had different answer categories so that it was not comparable across countries.

In some charts and overviews, we have combined countries to show broad regional differences in Europe. Although highly arbitrarily, we decided to define countries as being part of the North (Sweden, Norway, Finland, Denmark, Iceland), the West (Netherlands, Belgium, Luxembourg, Great Britain, Ireland, Northern Ireland, France, Germany, Austria, Switzerland), the South (Portugal, Spain, Italy, Greece, Malta), the East (Poland, Czech Republic, Slovak Republic, Hungary, Romania, Bulgaria, Croatia, Slovenia, Serbia, Bosnia Herzegovina, Montenegro, Macedonia, Albania), Former Soviet Union countries (Estonia, Latvia, Lithuania, Belarus, Ukraine, Moldova, Russia, Georgia, Azerbaijan, Armenia) and Turkey. Turkey was identified as a single country because it is the only Moslem country in Europe.

The countries abbreviations used, are the abbreviations used in international communications on the internet: Albania (al), Armenia (am), Austria (at), Azerbadjan (az), Belarus (by), Belgium (be), Bosnia Herzegovina (ba), Bulgaria (bg), Croatia (hr), Czech Republic (cz), Denmark (dk), Estonia (ee), Finland (fi), France (fr), Georgia (ge), Germany (de), Great Britain (gb), Greece (gr), Hungary (hu), Iceland (is), Ireland (ie), Italy (it), Latvia (lv), Lithuania (lt), Luxembourg (lu), Macedonia (mk), Malta (mt), Moldova (mo), Montenegro (mon), Netherlands (nl), Northern Ireland (nir), Norway (no), Poland (pl), Portugal (pt), Romania (ro), Russia (ru), Serbia (ser), Slovak Republic (sk), Slovenia (si), Spain (es), Sweden (se), Switzerland (ch), Turkey (tr), Ukraine (ua).

Finally, three levels of education (low, middle and high) are distinguished throughout the atlas. The distinction is based on a question about the highest level of education the respondent had reached. 'Low' level indicates inadequately completed elementary education, completed (compulsory) elementary education, and (compulsory) elementary education and basic vocational qualification. 'Middle' level education includes secondary, intermediate vocational qualification, secondary, intermediate general qualification and full secondary, maturity level certificate. A 'high' level of education means higher education lower-level tertiary certificate and upper-level tertiary certificate.

The European Values Study: a third wave, Sourcebook of the 1999/2000 European Values Study surveys, L. Halman, WORC Tilburg University (2001)
Human beliefs and values, a cross-cultural sourcebook based on the 1999-2002 values surveys, R. Inglehart, M. Basáñez, J. Díez-Medrano, L.Halman & R. Luijkx Eds. Siglo XXI Editores, Mexico (2004)
European Values Study 1999/2000, a third wave: Data, documentation and databases on CD-ROM, R. Luijkx, E. Brislinger & W. Zenk-Moeltgen, ZA-Information 52, 171-183 (2003)

Data on Europe

Geography and demography

Area

Country	sqeare kilometers
Russian Fed.	16995800
Turkey	770760
Ukraine	603700
France	545630
Spain	499542
Sweden	410934
Germany	349223
Norway	307860
Finland	305470
Poland	304465
Italy	294020
United Kingdom	241590
Romania	230340
Belarus	207600
Greece	130800
Bulgaria	110550
Serbia and Montenegro	102136
Iceland	100250
Hungary	92340
Portugal	91951
Azerbaijan	86100
Austria	82738
Czech Rep.	77276
Georgia	69700
Ireland	68890
Lithuania	65200
Latvia	63589
Croatia	56414
Bosnia and Herz.	51129
Slovak Rep.	48800
Estonia	43211
Denmark	42394
Switzerland	39770
Netherlands	33883
Moldova	33371
Belgium	30230
Armenia	28400
Albania	27398
Macedonia	24856
Slovenia	20151
Cyprus	9240
Luxembourg	2586
Malta	316

Capital city

Country	
Netherlands	Amsterdam
Turkey	Ankara
Greece	Athens
Azerbaijan	Baku (Baki)
Serbia and Montenegro	Belgrade
Germany	Berlin
Switzerland	Bern
Slovak Rep.	Bratislava
Belgium	Brussels
Romania	Bucharest
Hungary	Budapest
Moldova	Chisinau
Denmark	Copenhagen
Ireland	Dublin
Finland	Helsinki
Ukraine	Kiev (Kyyiv)
Portugal	Lisbon
Slovenia	Ljubljana
United Kingdom	London
Luxembourg	Luxembourg
Spain	Madrid
Belarus	Minsk
Russian Fed.	Moscow
Cyprus	Nicosia
Norway	Oslo
France	Paris
Czech Rep.	Prague
Iceland	Reykjavik
Latvia	Riga
Italy	Rome
Bosnia and Herz.	Sarajevo
Macedonia	Skopje
Bulgaria	Sofia
Sweden	Stockholm
Estonia	Tallinn
Georgia	T'bilisi
Albania	Tirana
Malta	Valletta
Austria	Vienna
Lithuania	Vilnius
Poland	Warsaw
Armenia	Yerevan
Croatia	Zagreb

Life expectancy

Country	age (years) for 2003
Switzerland	80
Sweden	80
Iceland	80
Italy	79
France	79
Spain	79
Norway	79
Greece	79
Netherlands	79
Malta	78
Germany	78
Belgium	78
Austria	78
United Kingdom	78
Finland	78
Luxembourg	78
Ireland	77
Cyprus	77
Denmark	77
Portugal	76
Slovenia	76
Czech Rep.	75
Macedonia	74
Slovak Rep.	74
Croatia	74
Serbia and Montenegro	74
Poland	74
Albania	72
Bosnia and Herz.	72
Hungary	72
Bulgaria	72
Turkey	72
Romania	71
Estonia	70
Lithuania	70
Latvia	69
Belarus	68
Russian Fed.	68
Armenia	67
Ukraine	67
Moldova	65
Georgia	65
Azerbaijan	63

Population

Country	in millions (July 2003)
Russian Fed.	144.5
Germany	82.4
Turkey	68.1
France	60.2
United Kingdom	60.1
Italy	58.0
Ukraine	48.1
Spain	40.2
Poland	38.6
Romania	22.3
Netherlands	16.2
Greece	10.7
Serbia and Montenegro	10.7
Belarus	10.3
Belgium	10.3
Czech Rep.	10.2
Portugal	10.1
Hungary	10.0
Sweden	8.9
Austria	8.2
Azerbaijan	7.8
Bulgaria	7.5
Switzerland	7.3
Denmark	5.4
Slovak Rep.	5.4
Finland	5.2
Georgia	4.9
Norway	4.5
Croatia	4.4
Moldova	4.4
Bosnia and Herz.	4.0
Ireland	4.0
Albania	3.6
Lithuania	3.6
Armenia	3.3
Latvia	2.3
Macedonia	2.0
Slovenia	1.9
Estonia	1.4
Cyprus	0.8
Luxembourg	0.5
Malta	0.4
Iceland	0.3

Net immigration rate

Country	per 1,000 population (2003)
Luxembourg	9.14
Ireland	3.57
Belarus	2.66
Austria	2.44
Netherlands	2.35
Malta	2.34
Slovenia	2.34
United Kingdom	2.20
Germany	2.18
Norway	2.09
Italy	2.07
Denmark	2.04
Greece	1.96
Croatia	1.61
Switzerland	1.37
Sweden	1.00
Spain	0.99
Belgium	0.97
Czech Rep.	0.97
Russian Fed.	0.91
Hungary	0.78
France	0.66
Finland	0.63
Slovak Rep.	0.53
Portugal	0.49
Cyprus	0.43
Bosnia and Herz.	0.32
Lithuania	0.14
Turkey	0.00
Moldova	-0.27
Ukraine	-0.41
Poland	-0.49
Romania	-0.6
Estonia	-0.71
Latvia	-1.19
Serbia and Montenegro	-1.38
Albania	-1.39
Macedonia	-1.46
Iceland	-2.26
Georgia	-2.30
Armenia	-3.15
Bulgaria	-4.58
Azerbaijan	-5.16

Fertility rate

Country	children born per women (2003)
Azerbaijan	2.34
Albania	2.22
Turkey	2.03
Iceland	1.98
Croatia	1.93
Malta	1.91
Ireland	1.89
Cyprus	1.88
France	1.85
Norway	1.80
Serbia and Montenegro	1.77
Macedonia	1.75
Moldova	1.74
Denmark	1.73
Bosnia and Herz.	1.71
Finland	1.70
Luxembourg	1.70
United Kingdom	1.66
Netherlands	1.65
Belgium	1.62
Armenia	1.56
Sweden	1.54
Georgia	1.51
Portugal	1.49
Switzerland	1.48
Lithuania	1.43
Austria	1.41
Germany	1.37
Poland	1.37
Romania	1.36
Greece	1.35
Belarus	1.34
Ukraine	1.34
Russian Fed.	1.33
Estonia	1.27
Slovenia	1.27
Italy	1.26
Spain	1.26
Hungary	1.25
Slovak Rep.	1.25
Latvia	1.20
Czech Rep.	1.18
Bulgaria	1.13

Size average household

Country

Azerbaijan	4.7
Turkey	4.6
Albania	4.3
Armenia	4.3
Macedonia	3.9
Georgia	3.8
Bosnia and Herz.	3.6
Serbia and Montenegro	3.6
Malta	3.2
Spain	3.2
Ukraine	3.2
Croatia	3.1
Cyprus	3.1
Poland	3.1
Slovenia	3.1
Greece	3.0
Ireland	3.0
Portugal	3.0
Slovak Rep.	2.9
Romania	2.8
Russian Fed.	2.8
Bulgaria	2.7
Czech Rep.	2.7
Latvia	2.7
Belarus	2.6
Hungary	2.6
Lithuania	2.6
Moldova	2.6
Austria	2.4
Belgium	2.4
Estonia	2.4
France	2.4
United Kingdom	2.4
Netherlands	2.3
Switzerland	2.3
Denmark	2.2
Finland	2.2
Germany	2.2
Norway	2.2
Sweden	2.1

Language

Country	main languages
Czech Rep.	Czech
United Kingdom	English, Welsh, Scottish form of Gaelic
Austria	German
Germany	German
Hungary	Hungarian 98.2%
Poland	Polish
Portugal	Portuguese (official), Mirandese (official - but locally used)
Ukraine	Ukrainian, Russian, Romanian
Albania	Albanian (Tosk is the official dialect), Greek
Armenia	Armenian 96%
Azerbaijan	Azerbaijani (Azeri) 89%
Belarus	Belarusian, Russian
Bulgaria	Bulgarian
Spain	Castilian Spanish 74%, Catalan 17%,
Croatia	Croatian 96%
Bosnia and Herz.	Croatian, Serbian, Bosnian
Denmark	Danish, Faroese, Greenlandic (an Inuit dialect), German (small minority), (English is the predominant second language)
Netherlands	Dutch (official language), Frisian (official language)
Belgium	Dutch (official) 60%, French (official) 40%
Ireland	English, Irish (Gaelic)
Estonia	Estonian (official), Russian
Finland	Finnish 93.4% (official), Swedish 5.9% (official)
France	French
Georgia	Georgian 71% (official), Russian 9%
Switzerland	German 63.7%, French 19.2%, Italian 7.6%
Greece	Greek 99% (official), English, French
Cyprus	Greek, Turkish
Iceland	Icelandic, English, Nordic languages, German widely spoken
Italy	Italian (official), German, French, Slovene
Latvia	Latvian (official), Lithuanian, Russian
Lithuania	Lithuanian (official), Polish, Russian
Luxembourg	Luxembourgish (national language), German and French (administrative languages)
Macedonia	Macedonian 70%, Albanian 21%
Malta	Maltese (official), English (official)
Moldova	Moldovan, Russian, Gagauz (a Turkish dialect)
Norway	Norwegian (official), (small Sami- and Finnish-speaking minorities)
Romania	Romanian (official), Hungarian, German
Russian Fed.	Russian, other
Serbia and Montenegro	Serbian 95%
Slovak Rep.	Slovak (official), Hungarian
Slovenia	Slovenian 91%, Serbo-Croatian 6%,
Sweden	Swedish (small Sami- and Finnish-speaking minorities)
Turkey	Turkish (official), Kurdish, Arabic, Armenian, Greek

Source: The main source used for the above data on Europe is www.nationmaster.com (which is based on the CIA World Factbook 2003). Other sources include: statistical yearbook of the Economic Commission for Europe 2003 (www.unece.org/stats/trends/), the International Labour Organization (www.ilo.org), Eurostat, CIA World Factbook, Center for International Research, Encyclopadia Britannica, and www.internetworldstats.com.

N.B. When a country is not listed, data for this nation was not available.
When data for Great Britain and Northern Ireland were not availeble, data for the United Kingdom is included.

Economics and Finance

Gross national income

Country	in billion euros
Germany	1617
United Kingdom	1233
France	1150
Italy	933
Spain	490
Netherlands	325
Switzerland	231
Sweden	222
Russian Fed.	211
Belgium	204
Austria	163
Turkey	139
Denmark	137
Poland	137
Norway	134
Finland	103
Greece	101
Portugal	91
Ireland	73
Czech Rep.	45
Hungary	41
Romania	33
Ukraine	29
Croatia	17
Slovak Rep.	17
Slovenia	16
Luxembourg	15
Belarus	11
Bulgaria	11
Lithuania	10
Cyprus	8
Iceland	7
Latvia	7
Azerbaijan	4
Bosnia and Herz.	4
Estonia	4
Malta	3
Albania	3
Georgia	3
Macedonia	3
Armenia	2
Moldova	1

Comparative price level

Country	2002 (EU 15 = 100)
Norway	144.7
Switzerland	144.4
Denmark	130.7
Iceland	130.6
Finland	122.7
Ireland	118.4
Sweden	117.3
United Kingdom	107.5
Germany	104.0
Netherlands	101.8
Austria	101.6
France	99.7
Luxembourg	99.7
Belgium	98.7
Italy	94.6
Cyprus	82.8
Spain	82.4
Greece	79.7
Portugal	73.5
Slovenia	72.6
Malta	71.9
Estonia	60.8
Poland	57.5
Hungary	54.8
Latvia	54.2
Czech Rep.	53.1
Lithuania	51.3
Turkey	48.9
Slovak Rep.	43.5
Bulgaria	40.2
Romania	39.5

GDP (per capita)

Country	per person (in euros) for 2003
Luxembourg	40258
Norway	27331
Switzerland	26576
Iceland	25059
Belgium	24273
Ireland	24146
Denmark	24036
Austria	23173
Netherlands	22590
Germany	21845
Sweden	21654
France	21574
Finland	21480
United Kingdom	21189
Italy	20906
Spain	17628
Portugal	16103
Slovenia	15955
Greece	15884
Malta	14189
Czech Rep.	12773
Hungary	11116
Slovak Rep.	10334
Estonia	9182
Croatia	8126
Russian Fed.	8124
Poland	8053
Latvia	7448
Belarus	7282
Lithuania	6978
Romania	6335
Turkey	5992
Bulgaria	5443
Macedonia	4269
Ukraine	3780
Albania	3650
Azerbaijan	3045
Armenia	3039
Georgia	2711
Moldova	2161
Serbia and Montenegro	1811
Bosnia and Herz.	1525

GDP (services)

Country	percentage in 2003
Belgium	74
United Kingdom	74
Malta	72
Netherlands	71
Denmark	71
France	71
Latvia	70
Greece	69
Luxembourg	69
Sweden	69
Germany	68
Portugal	68
Italy	68
Norway	67
Estonia	66
Austria	65
Iceland	65
Spain	65
Switzerland	64
Hungary	62
Finland	62
Slovak Rep.	61
Poland	61
Lithuania	61
Slovenia	61
Russian Fed.	60
Croatia	58
Macedonia	58
Bulgaria	58
Turkey	57
Czech Rep.	55
Georgia	55
Romania	50
Ireland	49
Moldova	49
Azerbaijan	47
Bosnia and Herz.	46
Belarus	45
Armenia	44
Serbia and Montenegro	38
Ukraine	35
Albania	24

General government expenditure

Country	percentage of GDP in 2003
Italy	106.2
Greece	103.0
Belgium	100.5
Cyprus	72.2
Malta	72.0
Austria	65.0
Germany	64.2
France	63.7
Portugal	59.4
Hungary	59.0
Netherlands	54.8
Sweden	51.8
Spain	50.8
Poland	45.4
Finland	45.3
Denmark	45.0
Slovak Rep.	42.8
Norway	42.0
United Kingdom	39.8
Czech Rep.	37.6
Ireland	32.0
Slovenia	27.1
Lithuania	21.9
Latvia	15.6
Estonia	5.8
Luxembourg	4.9

GDP (agriculture)

Country	percentage in 2003
Albania	49
Armenia	30
Moldova	28
Serbia and Montenegro	26
Ukraine	23
Azerbaijan	20
Georgia	20
Belarus	15
Romania	15
Bulgaria	14
Iceland	14 (12 is fishing)
Turkey	13
Macedonia	11
Croatia	9
Greece	8
Lithuania	8
Estonia	6
Russian Fed.	6
Ireland	5
Latvia	5
Slovak Rep.	5
Hungary	4
Finland	4
Spain	4
Czech Rep.	4
Poland	4
Portugalt	4
Slovenia	3
Netherlands	3
Denmark	3
France	3
Malta	3
Italy	2
Austria	2
Sweden	2
Switzerland	2
Norway	2
United Kingdom	1
Belgium	1
Germany	1
Luxembourg	1

GDP (industry)

Country	percentage in 2003
Ireland	46
Ukraine	42
Czech Rep.	41
Bosnia and Herz.	41
Belarus	40
Slovenia	36
Serbia and Montenegro	36
Poland	35
Romania	35
Russian Fed.	35
Slovak Rep.	34
Finland	34
Switzerland	34
Hungary	34
Austria	33
Azerbaijan	33
Croatia	33
Germany	31
Lithuania	31
Macedonia	31
Spain	31
Norway	31
Turkey	30
Italy	30
Luxembourg	30
Sweden	29
Portugal	29
Estonia	29
Bulgaria	29
Albania	27
Armenia	26
Denmark	26
France	26
Latvia	26
Netherlands	26
Malta	26
Georgia	25
United Kingdom	25
Belgium	24
Moldova	23
Greece	22
Iceland	21

Export products

Country	main products
Turkey	apparel, foodstuffs, textiles,
Cyprus	citrus, potatoes, pharmaceuticals (Greek Cypriot area)
Portugal	clothing and footwear, machinery, chemicals
Bulgaria	clothing, footwear, iron and steel
Armenia	diamonds, mineral products, foodstuffs
Italy	engineering products, textiles and clothing, production machinery
Ukraine	ferrous and nonferrous metals, fuel and petroleum products, chemicals
Iceland	fish and fish products, animal products, aluminum
Greece	food and beverages, manufactured goods, petroleum products
Macedonia	food, beverages, tobacco
Moldova	foodstuffs, textiles, machinery
Estonia	machinery and equipment, wood and paper, textiles, food products
Belgium	machinery and equipment, chemicals, diamonds
Netherlands	machinery and equipment, chemicals, fuels
Finland	machinery and equipment, chemicals, metals
Ireland	machinery and equipment, computers, chemicals
Belarus	machinery and equipment, mineral products, chemicals
Austria	machinery and equipment, motor vehicles and parts,
Hungary	machinery and equipment, other manufactures, food products
Luxembourg	machinery and equipment, steel products, chemicals
Denmark	machinery and instruments, meat and meat products, dairy products
Slovak Rep.	machinery and transport equipment, intermediate manufactured goods
Czech Rep.	machinery and transport equipment, intermediate manufacturers
Poland	machinery and transport equipment, intermediate manufactured goods
Malta	machinery and transport equipment, manufacturers
France	machinery and transportation equipment, aircraft
Switzerland	machinery, chemicals, metals
Sweden	machinery, motor vehicles, paper products
Spain	machinery, motor vehicles, foodstuffs
Germany	machinery, vehicles, chemicals
Serbia and Montenegro	manufactured goods, food and live animals
United Kingdom	manufactured goods, fuels, chemicals
Slovenia	manufactured goods, machinery and transport equipment, chemicals
Bosnia and Herz.	metals, clothing, wood products
Lithuania	mineral products, textiles and clothing, machinery and equipment
Azerbaijan	oil and gas
Norway	petroleum and petroleum products, machinery and equipment
Russian Fed.	petroleum and petroleum products, natural gas
Georgia	scrap metal, machinery, chemicals
Romania	textiles and footwear, metals and metal products, machinery and equipment
Albania	textiles and footwear, asphalt, metals and metallic ores
Croatia	transport equipment, textiles, chemicals
Latvia	wood and wood products, machinery and equipment, metals

Currency

Country	in 2003
Azerbaijan	Azerbaijani manat (AZM)
Belarus	Belarusian ruble (BYB/BYR)
United Kingdom	British pound (GBP)
Czech Rep.	Czech koruna (CZK)
Denmark	Danish krone (DKK)
Armenia	dram (AMD)
Estonia	Estonian kroon (EEK)
Austria	euro (EUR)
Finland	euro (EUR)
France	euro (EUR)
Germany	euro (EUR)
Greece	euro (EUR)
Ireland	euro (EUR)
Italy	euro (EUR)
Luxembourg	euro (EUR)
Netherlands	euro (EUR)
Portugal	euro (EUR)
Spain	euro (EUR)
Belgium	euro (EUR)
Hungary	forint (HUF)
Cyprus	Greek Cypriot area: Cypriot pound (CYP); Turkish Cypriot area: Turkish lira (TRL)
Ukraine	hryvnia (UAH)
Iceland	Icelandic krona (ISK)
Croatia	kuna (HRK)
Georgia	lari (GEL)
Latvia	Latvian lat (LVL)
Albania	lek (ALL)
Romania	leu (ROL)
Bulgaria	lev (BGL)
Lithuania	litas (LTL)
Macedonia	Macedonian denar (MKD)
Malta	Maltese lira (MTL)
Bosnia and Herz.	marka (BAM)
Moldova	Moldovan leu (MDL)
Serbia and Montenegro	new Yugoslav dinar (YUM); note - in Montenegro the euro is legal tender; in Kosovo both the euro and the Yugoslav dinar are legal (2002)
Norway	Norwegian krone (NOK)
Russian Fed.	Russian ruble (RUR)
Slovak Rep.	Slovak koruna (SKK)
Sweden	Swedish krona (SEK)
Switzerland	Swiss franc (CHF)
Slovenia	tolar (SIT)
Turkey	Turkish lira (TRL)
Poland	zloty (PLN)

Government and Society

Government type

Country	in 2003
Denmark	Constitutional monarchy
Luxembourg	Constitutional monarchy
Netherlands	Constitutional monarchy
Norway	Constitutional monarchy
Sweden	Constitutional monarchy
United Kingdom	Constitutional monarchy
Iceland	Constitutional republic
Albania	Emerging Democracy
Bosnia and Herz.	Emerging federal democratic republic
Belgium	Federal parliamentary democracy under a constitutional monach
Austria	Federal Republic
Germany	Federal Republic
Switzerland	Federal Republic
Russian Fed.	Federation
Bulgaria	Parliamentary democracy
Czech Rep.	Parliamentary democracy
Hungary	Parliamentary democracy
Latvia	Parliamentary democracy
Lithuania	Parliamentary democracy
Macedonia	Parliamentary democracy
Portugal	Parliamentary democracy
Slovak Rep.	Parliamentary democracy
Slovenia	Parliamentary democracy republic
Spain	Parliamentary monarchy
Estonia	Parliamentary republic
Greece	Parliamentary republic
Croatia	Presidential/parliamentary democracy
Armenia	Republic
Azerbaijan	Republic
Belarus	Republic
Cyprus	Republic
Finland	Republic
France	Republic
Georgia	Republic
Ireland	Republic
Italy	Republic
Malta	Republic
Moldova	Republic
Poland	Republic
Romania	Republic
Serbia and Montenegro	Republic
Ukraine	Republic
Turkey	Republican parliamentary democracy

Education level

Country	tertiary education (total students per 1000 population)
Finland	52
Poland	47
Slovenia	46
Spain	46
Belarus	44
Latvia	43
Estonia	42
Ireland	42
Norway	42
Austria	39
Russian Fed.	38
France	37
Lithuania	37
Iceland	36
Portugal	36
Belgium	35
Denmark	35
United Kingdom	34
Greece	31
Italy	31
Netherlands	31
Sweden	31
Bulgaria	30
Hungary	30
Ukraine	30
Georgia	28
Moldova	28
Slovak Rep.	27
Germany	25
Czech Rep.	24
Romania	24
Malta	22
Turkey	21
Croatia	19
Azerbaijan	18
Macedonia	18
Armenia	16
Cyprus	16
Serbia and Montenegro	16
Luxembourg	14
Switzerland	13
Albania	12
Bosnia and Herz.	1

Unemployment

Country	percentage of the labour force
Bosnia and Herz.	39.9
Macedonia	30.5
Serbia and Montenegro	27.9
Bulgaria	19.4
Slovak Rep.	19.2
Poland	18.2
Lithuania	17.0
Croatia	15.8
Georgia	15.8
Albania	14.5
Latvia	13.1
Estonia	12.6
Ukraine	11.1
Spain	10.5
Greece	10.2
Armenia	9.8
Italy	9.5
Finland	9.1
Russian Fed.	8.9
France	8.5
Turkey	8.5
Czech Rep.	8.1
Germany	7.9
Moldova	7.3
Belgium	6.6
Romania	6.6
Slovenia	5.9
Hungary	5.7
Malta	5.0
United Kingdom	4.8
Denmark	4.3
Portugal	4.1
Cyprus	4.0
Sweden	4.0
Ireland	3.7
Austria	3.6
Norway	3.6
Netherlands	2.7
Switzerland	2.6
Iceland	2.3
Belarus	2.1
Luxembourg	2.0
Azerbaijan	1.3

Religion

Country	dominant
United Kingdom	Angelican
Italy	Catholic (98%)
Malta	Catholic (98%)
Poland	Catholic (95%)
Portugal	Catholic (94%)
Spain	Catholic (94%)
Ireland	Catholic (91.6%)
Croatia	Catholic (87.8%)
Luxembourg	Catholic (87%)
Lithuania	Catholic (85%)
France	Catholic (83-88%)
Austria	Catholic (78%)
Belgium	Catholic (75%)
Slovenia	Catholic (70.8%)
Hungary	Catholic (67.5%)
Slovak Rep.	Catholic (60.3%)
Czech Rep.	Catholic (39.2%)
Netherlands	Catholic (31%)
Germany	Catholic and protestant (both 34%)
Turkey	Muslim (99.8 %)
Azerbaijan	Muslim (93.4%)
Albania	Muslim (70%)
Bosnia and Herz.	Muslim (40%)
Greece	Orthodox (98%)
Moldova	Orthodox (98%)
Romania	Orthodox (87%)
Bulgaria	Orthodox (83.8%)
Belarus	Orthodox (80%)
Cyprus	Orthodox (78%)
Ukraine	Orthodox (76%)
Russian Fed.	Orthodox (71.8%)
Macedonia	Orthodox (67%)
Georgia	Orthodox (65%)
Serbia and Montenegro	Orthodox (65%)
Armenia	Other
Denmark	Protestant (95%)
Finland	Protestant (89%)
Iceland	Protestant (87.1)
Sweden	Protestant (87%)
Norway	Protestant (86%)
Estonia	Protestant (78%)
Latvia	Protestant

Literacy

Country	percentage in 2003
Denmark	100.0
Finland	100.0
Luxembourg	100.0
Norway	100.0
Iceland	99.9
Estonia	99.8
Latvia	99.8
Poland	99.8
Ukraine	99.7
Belarus	99.6
Lithuania	99.6
Russian Fed.	99.6
Hungary	99.4
Moldova	99.1
France	99.0
Georgia	99.0
Germany	99.0
Netherlands	99.0
Sweden	99.0
Switzerland	99.0
United Kingdom	99.0
Armenia	98.6
Bulgaria	98.6
Italy	98.6
Croatia	98.5
Romania	98.4
Austria	98.0
Belgium	98.0
Ireland	98.0
Spain	97.9
Cyprus	97.6
Greece	97.5
Azerbaijan	97.0
Portugal	93.3
Serbia and Montenegro	93.0
Malta	92.8
Albania	86.5
Turkey	86.5

Total social security expenditure

Country	percentage of GDP - for 1996
Sweden	34.7
Denmark	33.0
Finland	32.3
France	30.1
Germany	29.7
Norway	28.5
Belgium	27.1
Netherlands	26.7
Austria	26.2
Switzerland	25.9
Luxembourg	25.2
Poland	25.1
Italy	23.7
United Kingdom	22.8
Greece	22.7
Croatia	22.3
Hungary	22.3
Spain	22.0
Slovak Rep.	20.9
Malta	20.6
Latvia	19.2
Portugal	19.0
Czech Rep.	18.8
Iceland	18.6
Ireland	17.8
Belarus	17.4
Estonia	17.1
Moldova	15.5
Lithuania	14.7
Bulgaria	13.2
Romania	12.4
Albania	10.9
Russian Fed.	10.4
Cyprus	10.3
Azerbaijan	8.4
Turkey	7.1

Internet users

Country	penetration (% population)
Sweden	76.6
Iceland	66.6
Netherlands	66.5
Denmark	62.5
Switzerland	62.0
United Kingdom	60.1
Germany	54.9
Finland	50.7
Norway	50.0
Italy	49.3
Austria	46.5
Latvia	40.4
France	38.7
Slovenia	38.4
Luxembourg	36.5
Belgium	36.2
Spain	34.5
Estonia	32.9
Ireland	32.8
Turkey	32.7
Malta	31.3
Czech Rep.	26.4
Slovak Rep.	25.6
Poland	23.5
Croatia	22.8
Cyprus	22.1
Lithuania	20.2
Portugal	19.2
Hungary	15.8
Greece	15.3
Belarus	14.2
Romania	10.2
Bulgaria	8.3
Serbia and Montenegro	8.1
Armenia	5.1
Macedonia	4.9
Russian Fed.	4.1
Azerbaijan	3.6
Moldova	3.6
Georgia	3.3
Bosnia and Herz.	2.3
Ukraine	1.9
Albania	1.0

Biggest political party

Country	party name
Turkey	Adalet ve Kalkinma Partisi (Justice and Development Party)
Cyprus	Anorthotikon Komma Ergazemenou Laou (Progressive Party of the Working People)
Sweden	Arbetarepartiet-Socialdemokraterna (Workers' Party Social-Democrats)
Ukraine	Blok Viktora Iushchenka Nasha Ukraina (Viktor Yushchenko's Bloc Our Ukraine)
Czech Rep.	Česká strana sociálné demokratická (Czech Social Democratic Party)
Luxembourg	Chrëschtlich Sozial Vollekspartei (Christian Social People's Party)
Netherlands	Christen Democratisch Appèl (Christian-Democratic Appeal)
Azerbaijan	Democratic Party of Artsakh
Serbia and Montenegro	Demokratska Opozicija Srbije (Democratic Opposition of Serbia)
Norway	Det Norske Arbeiderparti (Norwegian Labour Party)
Estonia	Eesti Keskerakond (Estonian Centre Party)
Ireland	Fianna Fáil (Soldiers of Destiny)
Hungary	FIDESZ-MDF (Fidesz - Hungarian Citizens' Party and Hungarian Democratic Forum
Armenia	Hayastani Hanrapetakan Kusaktsutyun (Republican Party of Armenia)
Slovak Rep.	Hnutie za Demokraticke Slovensko (Movement for a Democratic Slovakia)
Latvia	Jaunais laiks (New Era)
Poland	Koalicja Sojuszu Lewicy Demokratycznej i Unii Pracy (Coalition of the Alliance of Democratic Left and the Union of Labour)
Russian Fed.	Kommunisticheskaya Partiya Rossiiskoi Federatsii (Communist Party of the Russian Federation)
Belarus	Kommunisticheskaya Partya Belarusi (Communist Party of Belarus)
Italy	La Casa delle Libertà (House of Freedom)
United Kingdom	Labour Party
Slovenia	Liberalna Demokracija Slovenije (Liberal Democracy of Slovenia)
Bulgaria	Natsionalnoto Dvizhenie Simeon Vtori (National Movement Simeon the Second)
Austria	Österreichische Volkspartei (Austrian People's Party)
Greece	Panellino Socialistiko Kinima (Pan-Hellenic Socialist Movement)
Albania	Partia Socialiste ë Shqipërisë (Socialist Party of Albania)
Spain	Partido Popular (People's Party)
Portugal	Partido Social Democrata (Social Democrat Party)
Malta	Partit Nazzjonalista (Nationalist Party)
Romania	Polul Democrat-Social din România (Democratic Social Pole of Romania)
Georgia	Sak'art'velos Mokalaketa Kavshiri (Citizens' Union of Georgian)
Switzerland	Schweizerische Volkspartei (Swiss People's Party)
Croatia	SDP i HSLS (SDP and HSLS, Social Democratic Party of Croatia and Croatian Social Liberal Party
Iceland	Sjálfstæðisflokkurinn (Independence Party)
Lithuania	Socialdemokratin Coalicija (Social Democratic Coalition)
Germany	Sozialdemokratische Partei Deutschlands (Social Democratic Party of Germany)
Bosnia and Herz.	Srpska Demokratska Stranka (Serbian Democratic Party)
Finland	Suomen Keskusta/Centern i Finland (Finnish Centre)
France	Union pour un Mouvement Populaire (Union for the Presidential Majority)
Denmark	Venstre, Danmarks liberale parti (Left, Liberal Party of Denmark)
Belgium	Vlaamse Liberalen en Democraten (Flemish Liberals and Democrats)
Moldova	Yedinstvo (Unity)
Macedonia	Za Makedonija zaedno (Together for Macedonia)

Prison population

Country	per 100,000 population
Belarus	550
Russian Fed.	460
Ukraine	348
Azerbaijan	262
Estonia	233
Latvia	211
Lithuania	204
Moldova	164
Romania	154
Czech Rep.	150
Georgia	116
Hungary	109
Bulgaria	98
Slovak Rep.	92
Spain	90
Portugal	85
Ireland	84
Armenia	72
Austria	67
Germany	65
Macedonia	59
France	56
Italy	51
Finland	50
Switzerland	48
Netherlands	44
Denmark	43
Sweden	41
Slovenia	37
Turkey	34
Cyprus	31
Norway	30
Iceland	28

Committed international homicides

Country	per 100,000 population
Russian Fed.	21.9
Albania	18.3
Luxembourg	14.0
Estonia	13.7
Belarus	11.5
Latvia	11.2
Netherlands	10.9
Sweden	10.4
Ukraine	9.6
Lithuania	9.0
Romania	7.4
Bulgaria	6.2
Croatia	6.0
Moldova	6.0
Macedonia	5.4
Turkey	4.9
Georgia	4.7
Italy	4.4
Armenia	4.1
Slovenia	4.1
Azerbaijan	4.0
Denmark	4.0
France	3.7
Hungary	3.5
Germany	3.4
Poland	3.4
Portugal	3.3
Cyprus	3.1
Spain	2.9
Greece	2.8
Belgium	2.7
Czech Rep.	2.7
Norway	2.7
Slovak Rep.	2.4
Switzerland	2.3
Malta	2.0
Ireland	1.4
Finland	0.7
Iceland	0.0
United Kingdom	14.3 (Scotland)
	6.4 (Northern Ireland)
	2.8 (England and Wales)

List of contributors

Wil Arts is a professor of General and Theoretical Sociology and head of the Sociology Department at Tilburg University

Joost Beelenkamp is a designer, and owner of Beelenkamp Ontwerpers, a design company in Tilburg, The Netherlands

Joyce van Belkom is a freelance photographer, working for various magazines and newspapers; she is represented by Hollandse Hoogte

Ralf Bodelier is a journalist and writer based in Tilburg, The Netherlands

Paul Dekker is a professor of Civil Society at Tilburg University and a senior research fellow at the Social and Cultural Planning Bureau in The Hague

Wim van de Donk is chairman of the Scientific Council of the Government Policy in The Hague and a professor of Public Administration at Tilburg University

Peter Ester is a professor of General and Theoretical Sociology and director of the Institute of Labour Studies (OSA) at Tilburg University

Loek Halman is an associate professor of Sociology at Tilburg University, secretary to the Board and the Steering Committee of EVS, and program director of the European Values Study

Ruud Luijkx is lecturer in Sociology at Tilburg University and data manager for the European Values Study

Carla van den Ouweland is a freelance designer working on a regular basis for Beelenkamp Ontwerpers, a design company in Tilburg

Fred van Raaij is a professor of Economical Psychology at the Faculty of Social and Behavioural Sciences at Tilburg University

Theo Schepens is associate professor of Theology at the Faculty of Theology at Tilburg University.

Pieter Siebers is a spokesman and vice head at the Office of Public and External affairs at Tilburg University

Coen Tuerlings is a media designer and owner of GO design, a media production company in Tilburg, The Netherlands

Wilfred Uunk is an assistant professor of Social Cultural Sciences at Tilburg University, The Netherlands

Willem Witteveen is a professor in Law at the Department of Jurisprudence and History of Law, Faculty of Law at Tilburg University

Marga van Zundert is a science information officer at Tilburg University and freelance science writer

Received

Mission College Library

169.00

Received

FEB 2 2 2006

Mission College Library

169.00